910·91

extreme places

highest • hottest • largest • coldest • wettest • deepest • driest

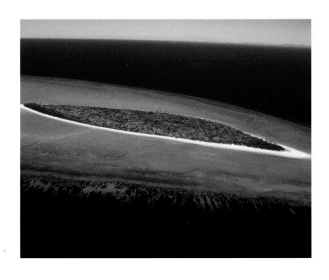

extreme places

highest • hottest • largest • coldest • wettest • deepest • driest

Authors: David Atkinson, Donna Dailey, Paul Deegan, Jane Egginton, Adele Evans, Mark Eveleigh, Mike Gerrard, Will Gray, Beth Hall, Clare Jones, Nick Middleton, Melissa Shales, Martin Symington, Janet Waltham, Steve Watkins and Paul Wilson

Managing Editor: Isla Love
Senior Editor: Donna Wood
Senior Designer: Alison Fenton
Picture Research: Carol Walker and Sian Lloyd
Picture Repro: Michael Moody
Copy-editor: Sharon Amos
Proofreader: Helen Ridge
Production Controller: Helen Brown

Produced by AA Publishing
© Copyright AA Media Limited 2011
First published 2007

ISBN: 978-0-7495-7160-3 (T)
ISBN: 978-0-7495-7161-0 (SS)

Published by AA Publishing (a trading name of AA Media Limited, whose registered office is Fanum House, Basing View, Basingstoke RG21 4EA; registered number 06112600).

A04699

Colour separation by MRM Graphics Limited, Winslow, Buckinghamshire
Printed in China by C & C Offset Printing Co. Ltd

www.theAA.com/shop

earth

Yukon 8
Göreme 12
Ngorongoro Crater 16
Salar de Uyuni 20
Patagonia 24
Atacama Desert 30
Grand Canyon 34
Guilin Hills 40

water

Iguassu Falls 46
Okavango Delta 50
Amazon River 56
Fjords of Norway 60
Lake Titicaca 64
Great Barrier Reef 68
River Ganges 74
Cape of Good Hope 78

fire

Mount Etna 84
Namib Desert 88
Sahara Desert 94
Yellowstone Geysers 98
Volcanoes National Park 102
Australian Outback 106
Death Valley 112
Krakatoa 116

ice

Greenland 122
Yakutia 126
Alaska 130
Baltoro Glacier 136
Iceland 140
Antarctic Peninsula 146
Lapland 150

air

Gobi Desert 156
Kilimanjaro 162
US Midwest 166
Everest and the Himalaya 170
Wadi Rum 174
Tibet 178
Peruvian Andes 182

life

Borneo 190
South Georgia 194
Madagascar 198
Central Tokyo 204
Galápagos Islands 208
Yosemite 214
Serengeti 218

introduction

What makes a place 'extreme'? We wanted to know the answer to that very question and so we went to the people who know. Our contributors include travel writers, adventurers and explorers, as well as a meteorologist (who else would we ask to tell us about the coldest inhabited place on the planet?) and a mountaineer. Each of our contributors has spent time in the place they have written about and so can tell us what it is really like to be there. Between them, they have been to just about every country in the world.

Each of the six chapters in this book has a theme which reflects the nature of the places in the chapter. In *Earth* we cover amazing and bizarre landscapes, whether on or below ground, including the Grand Canyon and the stark (and distinctly arid), Atacama Desert. In *Water*, our authors explore waterfalls and vast expanses of water, as well as landscapes and life which have been primarily shaped by water. The places range from the dramatic and treacherous coastline of the Cape of Good Hope to the spirituality of India's River Ganges.

In *Fire*, you'll find not only places which are very hot (and they don't come much hotter than Death Valley), but also places which are very dry or geo-active, such as the geysers of Yellowstone National Park. *Ice* speaks for itself. Very cold or snowy and icy landscapes define this chapter, yet even within this boundary there is great variety, from the geysers of Iceland to the grizzlies of Alaska. In many of the places in the *Ice* chapter, it is the survival story of the people and their animals which captures the imagination.

Our definition for the places in *Air* was that they had to be high up, windy or both. For example, the US Midwest, with its frequent tornadoes and isolated farms, really is an extreme landscape in which to eke out a living. Equally as awe-inspiring are the world's highest mountains, Kilimanjaro and Everest, which need no introduction. And finally, to *Life*. For us, 'life' had to mean plenty of it, and so we have sought out places which are absolutely teeming with it. South Georgia, isolated in the middle of the Southern Ocean and arguably the most dramatic-looking island in the world, is positively overrun with penguins and seals, whereas downtown Tokyo teems with life of a very different kind.

And finally, we hope you enjoy discovering these extreme places as much as we have enjoyed researching them.

earth

Yukon 8

Göreme 12

Ngorongoro Crater 16

Salar de Uyuni 20

Patagonia 24

Atacama Desert 30

Grand Canyon 34

Guilin Hills 40

Yukon

Throughout the upper reaches of the park, hundreds of cracked-ice glacial fingers inch their way down into the valleys before melting into the freezing Alsek River

The Yukon may not be as well known as Alaska, but its rugged, beautiful, and uncompromising landscape sets it apart – even from its famous neighbor. Located in the northwest of Canada and shaped like a delta wing pointing out toward the coast, the Yukon could easily have been the original inspiration for the word wilderness. It has an astonishing array of mountains, including Canada's highest peak, Mount Logan, the mighty Yukon River, grizzly bears, caribou, and enough other wildlife to keep even the most avid spotters glued to their binoculars.

For those of us who live in normally populated places, it is hard to grasp just how much open uninhabited space there is in the Yukon. The country is not far shy of the size of Spain, yet it is home to only 30,000 people. Around two-thirds of the population live in Whitehorse, the state capital, leaving what amounts to barely a small town's worth of people sprinkled throughout the rest of the territory. This isn't the place to expect traffic jams.

It wasn't always as quiet. One August day in 1896, Skookum Jim Mason, George Carmack and several friends were looking for gold in Rabbit Creek when they stumbled upon deposits in the stream bed. Word of the find spread quickly and within months the legendary Klondike Gold Rush was underway. It was by no means all wealth and glory. Prospectors faced an arduous and dangerous journey to get to Dawson City, the base for reaching

Klondike. After a punishing trek lugging masses of equipment and provisions along the mountainous Chilkoot Trail from the Alaskan port of Skagway, the gold rushers had to build their own boats for the 460-mile journey down the Yukon River from Whitehorse to Dawson. Many people lost their lives in the treacherous rapids en route. By 1901, the rush was all but over, a literal flash in the pan, and, predictably, only a tiny proportion of the 100,000 people who came here to find gold left with any tangible reward.

Dawson City remains and with its crooked wooden boardwalks, creaky swing-door saloons and slight air of dilapidated grandeur, it is an evocative reminder of the hope the rush inspired. Down the main street, former ladies parlors and signs banning weapons and explosives from bars also hint at the wild-living, often lawless characters who made the Gold Rush an exciting and extremely edgy time to be in the Yukon. Gold still plays a big part in the community, and there are several claims nearby where hopeful visitors can try their hand at panning. The lottery-winning thrill of suddenly seeing a few golden flecks sparkling among the silt shows how easy it still is to catch gold fever.

Retracing the route of the historic Gold Rush river journey from Whitehorse to Dawson can become the basis of a wonderful two-week canoe and camping trip, which takes you right to the heart of this spectacular region. Just in case you were wondering, some of the worst rapids have since been blasted to make for smoother waters. The Yukon River writhes through the territory for 1,980 miles – to give you some idea of just how far you are from civilization, there are only four road bridges along its entire length.

En route to Dawson, the river crosses 50-mile long Lake Laberge and passes several old encampments and paddle steamer wrecks from the Rush heyday. Along the shoreline, black bears and grizzly bears roam in search of berries while golden eagles soar overhead. Fortunate paddlers may find their path momentarily blocked by moose swimming across the river. At times, especially as you near Dawson City, the current slacks sufficiently to let the canoe float aimlessly downstream, a perfect moment for closing your eyes and listening to the sounds of nature at her most sublime.

The southwestern part of the Yukon, on the Alaskan border, is almost wholly protected within the Kluane National Park, established in 1972 and now a UNESCO World Heritage Site. Together with several adjoining parks in Alaska and British Columbia, it forms the largest protected natural area in the world. In among the sea of glaciers and snow-capped mountains of the St Elias range, lies 19,550ft Mount Logan, the highest peak in Canada. Throughout the upper reaches of the park, hundreds of cracked-ice glacial fingers inch their way down into the valleys before melting into the freezing Alsek River. Some of the valley glaciers in particular are of mammoth proportions, including the Lowell Glacier and Kaskawulsh Glacier. In spring, when the winter blanket of ice and snow recedes, scrubby tundra runs into broad alpine meadows, ideal feeding grounds for the lumbering grizzly and black bears. Among the other most notable inhabitants are Dall's sheep, with their trademark large spiral horns: the park is home to the last remaining flocks on Earth of this rare creature.

Although the Yukon may have only a handful of roads, they offer some of the best wilderness driving in North America. The Top of the World Highway takes you westward from Dawson City to the Alaskan border, offering spectacular mountain views and many switchback corners. More experienced adventure drivers can head into the Arctic Circle up the truly untamed Dempster Highway, a 417-mile dead-end route from Dawson City to Inuvik in the neighboring Northwest Territories. Surrounded by arctic tundra, it is Canada's most northerly highway and gravel-surfaced for almost its entire length; not one for your standard rental car. You are more likely to see bears than other vehicles and gas stations are equally rare, so careful planning for this trip is essential. The majestic upsweep of glacier-carved peaks funnels the route northward through the Ogilvie Mountains and Richardson Mountains and on toward the immense, wildlife-rich Mackenzie Delta, Canada's largest. Fed by several major rivers, including the mighty Mackenzie – North America's second longest after the Mississippi – the delta is a watery maze of countless lakes and three main channels, interspersed with vast tracts of black spruce forest. Like most of the Yukon, it is the very essence of wild.

TOKYO 8330 M

MOSCOW 6331 M

PARIS 3670 M

Göreme

Folds of soft rock pour across the valley like gentle waves. Surreal honeycomb pillars and clusters of conical formations rise upward. Cave dwellings cling to the sides, and subterranean cities lie below. The bizarre and beguiling landscape of Cappadocia is a geological masterpiece carved and sculpted by the ravages of wind, rain, and time. At the heart of this lunar landscape in the central Anatolian Plateau, in the heart of the Pasa Bagi, or Fairy Chimneys Valley, is the town of Göreme. Here, the rock-hewn houses are still inhabited, and you can sip traditional apple tea from the terrace of a café carved into the face of the rock.

> The bizarre and beguiling landscape of Cappadocia is a lunar landscape; a geological masterpiece carved and sculpted by the ravages of wind, rain, and time

The weird and wonderful landscape of the Cappadocia National Park, a UNESCO World Heritage Site in central Turkey, was created millions of years ago by two violent volcanic eruptions. Mount Ercyies (12,765ft) and Mount Hasan (10,662ft) spewed vast lava streams across 15,000 square miles. Fire-broken rocks, blown apart by exploding gases, deposited showers of ash. Over time, these consolidated, forming several different layers, most significantly a soft under layer called tufa and a harder outer layer of basalt. Wind and rain blasted the softer underlying tufa through cracks in the basalt. This continuous process of erosion ate away at the soft rock, gradually altering its shape and creating one of the most peculiar natural rock gardens to be seen on Earth, full of amazing fungi-like and phallic formations.

Göreme is surrounded by the results of this erosion, and you can wander through a surrealist moonscape of giant chess pawns. Eerie formations tower above, and all around you corrugated hills flow like whipped marshmallow, dotted with chimneys like tall flat-capped mushrooms. In the nearby Derbent, or Pink Valley, massive pastel pink and honey-colored boulders sit beneath yet more chimneys. Legend has it that one night when the moon was full the locals saw beings inside the conical pillars and named them the Fairy Chimneys.

Adding to the extraterrestrial feel of the place is the kaleidoscope of dreamy colors that comes magically to life as the sun sets and rises. Depending on the temperature at which the lava solidified, rocks can be dusty red or creamy white, merging with mustard yellows and sandy browns.

The landscape looks every bit a place of fantasy. It seems almost unreal that anyone should live here. But for centuries people have been taking refuge in the rocks, digging themselves troglodyte cave homes and finding sanctuary by burrowing deep into their folds. The Göreme Open Air Museum, situated not far from the village, reveals how extensive their excavations were. A monastic network of more than 30 rock-hewn churches and chapels, carved by early Christians who were fleeing Roman persecution, lies behind inconspicuous openings in the rock.

What seem like small scarred gouges in the rock face lead into an intricate complex of dimly lit passages. Some are just high enough to stand in while others require you to scramble, stoop, and crawl. Huge millstones, once used to block the passages in times of danger, remain at the doorways. Inside this extensive

religious campus, beautiful Byzantine frescoes from the ninth to the thirteenth century adorn the church walls, depicting scenes of primitive pagan imagery as well as some biblical tableaux.

More than 40 different communities existed beneath the surface in a labyrinth of subterranean cities where thousands of residents could retreat from marauding enemies. Derinkuyu is one of the largest. Carved 18 stories deep into the ground, it was once home to 20,000 people, the equivalent of a small market town bustling with everyday life.

At Kaymakli, one of the other elaborate cities unearthed, you can still explore five stories. Discreet entrances in the rock give way to complex underground systems with air shafts, wells, chimneys, grain stores, and even stables. Look carefully at the walls and you may find a deeply ingrained handprint in the rock face, a ghostly reminder of past inhabitants.

Many of the best cave dwellings can be found within a triangle formed by the villages of Göreme, Urgup, and the hilltop fortress town of Uchisar. This natural rocky citadel is built around a dramatic jutting promontory, a crumbling volcanic outcrop with far-reaching views across the park. From up here this improbable landscape looks like it could belong to another planet. This is one of the highest look-out points you will be able to get to, unless you take to the skies and float peacefully above the deep-cut ravines in a hot-air balloon at sunrise. Letting yourself drift whichever way the wind dictates, you can hover in the canyons, sidle up to the rocky pillars for closer inspection and float sedately upward to appreciate awesome 360-degree panoramic views. Below, lazy birds ride the thermals, and the faint but

audible cry of the muezzin provides an eerie dawn wake-up call for the rest of the world.

Surprisingly, although this volcanic landscape can seem extremely inhospitable, its mineral-rich soil is excellent for growing fruit and vegetables. Lush fertile plains and valleys merge in a patchwork of emerald greens. Close by to Göreme is Pigeon Valley where thousands of dovecotes have been carved in the soft tufa wherever space allowed, including abandoned caves and the walls of collapsed churches. Their sheer numbers are astonishing, and some farmers insist that the reputation of Cappadocian fruits as the sweetest in Turkey is entirely down to the wonderfully rich fertilizing properties of pigeon droppings.

This is a beguiling landscape, both above ground and below. Cappadocia is a living geological phenomenon sculpted by the elements and one that will continue to shape and reform before your very eyes.

Ngorongoro Crater

To gaze down into Tanzania's Ngorongoro Crater is like stumbling upon Sir Arthur Conan Doyle's fictional *Lost World* – but made real, here in the very heart of Africa. This is where humankind began, and this is where, on the fertile floor of the crater, the wildlife of East Africa seems to congregate as if drawn back to some primal place. It's as if they are searching for a time when they alone roamed the Earth, before one species evolved to rule them: humankind. In fact, examples of the earliest known human tools and skeletons have been found just a few miles from Ngorongoro, at the Olduvai Gorge.

The most savage predators are the packs of hyenas, which roam around the crater floor like gangs of muggers terrorizing the neighborhood

The Ngorongoro Crater is the largest unbroken and unflooded volcanic caldera on Earth. To reach it, visitors must drive through the Ngorongoro Conservation Area, which is about the size of Crete, and up to the edge to pause and gaze into the giant bowl. Gaze into and across it, for the other side is up to 10 miles distant. Gaze down, too, 2,000ft or so to the crater floor far below, filled with a microcosm of East African flora and fauna: grassland, soda lakes, swamps, forest, watering-holes, and wildlife.

Walk or drive into the almost perfectly circular crater and you are descending into the world of the animals. No humans live here; instead it's home to an estimated 30,000 creatures, including the largest concentration of predators in Africa. This is their world, not ours. The Masai still lead their cattle into the crater from time to time, to graze and to gain sustenance from the salt licks around

About three million years ago Ngorongoro was an active volcano, a mountain thought to have been higher than even Kilimanjaro – at 19,340ft the highest point in the vast African continent. Then Africa blew its top. The volcano erupted so violently that it thundered in on itself, and created what should technically be called the Ngorongoro caldera, a collapsed volcano. However, the name Ngorongoro Crater has stuck.

The origins of the name Ngorongoro are as mysterious as this lost world. Was it the name of a tribe, the Gorongoro, defeated by the Masai in a battle in the crater? Did it come from the words for a grinding stone or a bowl, both of which it is said to resemble? Or was it named for the rhythmic sound that the bells of the cattle make as the animals walk along, like a tuneful Masai version of 'ding-dong'?

The wild animals in the crater are surprisingly silent, for noise betrays their presence. The most savage predators are the packs of hyenas, which roam around the crater floor like gangs of muggers terrorizing the neighborhood. Gazelle and antelope keep a constant watch for them. Some animals are absent altogether. No giraffes lurch their way across the crater floor, for the sides of the caldera are too steep for them to negotiate on their spindly legs. Down here you find only bull elephants, probably for a similar reason – the young elephants are not dexterous enough to make their way down, so they stay outside with the females. The bull elephants congregate in the Lerai Forest in the south of the crater, and lumber over to one of the watering holes to bathe and trumpet.

Ngorongoro is no prison. The animals are free to come and go, and populations increase during times of migration. Those that remain on the floor of the crater stay there because they choose to. And at night when the sun goes down and the whole crater is cast into a giant shadow, the last of the human visitors climb back out to their own world. They stay in the campsites and lodges that perch high on the rim of the caldera and which afford amazing views over and into the crater.

A row of softly flickering lights shows the human herds congregating for safety and sustenance. Back on the crater floor, down in the darkness of Ngorongoro, the night world comes to life, and the lions roar.

Lake Makat. But even the Masai keep a watchful eye out for predators, especially for the several prides of lions, the undisputed kings of the crater, including the magnificent black-maned males that you are unlikely to find anywhere else. Drive along the rough roads that weave across the crater floor and you may come across the lions lounging on rocks at the side of the track, seemingly oblivious to the presence of man, with the relaxed confidence that only a king can display. Further on, wallowing in swampy water, may be hippos, yawning and snorting and splashing, or sinking beneath the surface. Here too are buffaloes; the most unpredictable of creatures, always to be treated with caution.

All of the 'big five' of African game species – lions, leopards, elephant, buffalo and rhino – can be found cupped in the crater's protective hand. Herds of zebra and wildebeest roam, gazelle too, and warthog. There are hundreds of bird species, many of which are not found anywhere outside the crater. Oxpeckers or tick birds graze on the backs of the rare black rhino, which you have a better chance of seeing in the Ngorongoro Crater than anywhere else in Africa.

Until relatively recently the future looked extremely bleak for the black rhino, as poachers hunted them almost to the brink of extinction. But helped by the unique atmosphere afforded by protected areas such as Ngorongoro, the numbers are slowly recovering. However, there are still only about three to four thousand of these prehistoric beasts left in the world.

Salar de Uyuni

Flat and blindingly white as far as the eye can see, the view from the middle of the world's largest salt flat, Salar de Uyuni, will either leave you feeling liberated or – more likely – overwhelmed, a small and insignificant speck on the face of the Earth. At more than 3,800 square miles, the salt flat, in the southwest corner of Bolivia, is half the size of Wales and is visible from the NASA International Space Station. It's big, very big. And standing there small and exposed, way out in the middle of the flat, feeling the crunch of the crusty salt beneath your feet and surrounded by more sky than you have ever seen in your entire life, you are likely to feel that this is quite unlike any other wilderness experience to be found on the planet.

The surface water on the blindingly white salt acts like a gigantic mirror, perfectly reflecting the cloud formations and leaving you free to wander in an endless sky

Like most of Bolivia, the salt flat is set at dizzying heights, standing around 11,975ft above sea level, near the border with Chile. It was created around 12,000 years ago by the receding waters of what was once the vast and prehistoric Lake Minchin, which covered the entire Altiplano, the extensive Andean high plateau. The Salar de Uyuni's water subsequently evaporated leaving 11 thick layers of salt, each around 20–30ft in depth. It won't take you long to realize how it happened: the scorching high-altitude sun, in cahoots with the reflective surface, can burn unprotected skin within minutes. If, in a moment of sun-kissed euphoria, you become tempted to try hiking across the salt flat, be warned: it stretches for more than 75 miles at its widest

point and, tragically, several people with broken-down vehicles are known to have met their end while endeavouring to attempt just such a feat.

Access requires a four-wheel-drive vehicle and an experienced driver: once you wander off the handful of main tracks, which is surprisingly easy due to their indistinct nature, things can become a little sticky. Beneath the crunchy surface layer lies a clinging, clay-like gloop, which can devour wheels and, with time, even complete vehicles. Explorers seeking access on mountain bikes have found that their over-enthusiasm for taking a route as the crow flies results in several hours of pulling and shoving their increasingly sludge-caked steeds in order to reach the edge.

To get out onto the salt flat, most visitors opt to join three- or four-day tours based out of the nearest town, the isolated Uyuni. Inhabited largely by the indigenous Aymara and Quechua Indians, it is a place very much in keeping with the arid, windswept surroundings – a staging post rather than a destination. The Aymara and Quechua people – separated by language rather than tribe – are widespread through the high Andes, and their origin can be traced back to around two thousand years ago, long before the Inca arrived in the region.

It is possible to go out onto the salt flat at any time of year. The winter months are generally graced with clear blue skies, but the summer months bring the floods, covering the entire salt flat in a very shallow layer of shimmering water. Although this can be a riskier period for driving as the surface softens, it is a truly magical time to venture out onto the salt, and the visual rewards can be completely staggering. The surface water lying calm as a millpond on top of the blindingly white salt acts like a gigantic mirror, perfectly reflecting the spectacular cloud formations and leaving you free to wander in what appears to be an endless sky.

A handful of rocky islands covered in towering cactus plants straight out of a B-movie Western are dotted around the lake. They offer superb vantage points over the vastness of this salty expanse. The most popular is Isla de los Pescadores, close to the middle, which rises more than 330ft above the salt. Scattered around it are ruins and tunnels from the ancient Tiwanaku and Inca civilizations. They make for some interesting exploration

while waiting to watch the sunset, which is for many the prime reason for coming to the island.

A bizarre treat for those who may be on the lookout for unusual experiences is the Salt Hotel, set in the middle of the salt flat and made entirely out of salt blocks, except for its thatched roof. It cannot be said to offer five-star facilities by any stretch of the imagination, but you do get to sleep in your very own salt bed. If you ever want to hear deafening silence or see real darkness, this is the ideal place. It can be a quite unsettling experience at first, but once your eyes adjust, you can look upward at a starry extravaganza that is guaranteed to take your breath away.

The hotel is a relatively new attempt to extract some wealth from the salt and is in stark contrast to the rudimentary salt mining or, more accurately, digging, which has been going on for decades. Some estimates put the Salar's salt supplies at around 10 billion tons, and the small, desperately poor desert town of Colchani, over on the southeastern shore, grew up around the business. On the salt flat near the town are many neat rows of conical salt piles, dug out by the gnarled sun-dried hands of men whose leathery weatherbeaten faces appear much older than their true age. There is little monetary reward for their efforts. On the one hand, you can't help but feel that they are trapped here, too far away from anywhere else and too poor to change things. On the other, the attraction of living and working in such a startlingly wild place and being essentially free could well have its own appeal.

The Salar de Uyuni is in itself well worth the lengthy journey from La Paz, the Bolivian capital, but there are many other wonders to see in the region. Further south there are volcanoes to climb, spouting geysers, boiling mud pools, and two outstanding lakes. Laguna Verde, with its bright green, magnesium-rich water, sits at the base of Licancábur Volcano while nearby Laguna Colorada, with its algae-laden, reddish brown water is home to tens of thousands of pink flamingos.

When you finally make your way back to La Paz, you will be left in no doubt whatsoever that you have been privileged to see one of the wildest, least inhabited, and most stunning regions on Earth. And the salt on your food will never taste quite the same again.

Patagonia

Tumultuous, wild, and at times unforgiving, Patagonia is a mighty land of deep fissured glaciers, enchanting blue and green lakes, and sky-piercing granite mountains. Uncluttered by the influence of human habitation, its wilderness will grip your imagination so tightly that, no matter how much or little time you spend here, you long to return. This narrowing finger at the very bottom of South America is actually part of two countries, Chile and Argentina, though it seems to rest most easily with its own Patagonia tag. Indeed, many people in the region see themselves as *Patagonicos* first and foremost. Once you have made the effort to get there – it's a three- or four-hour flight from either Buenos Aires or Santiago, both to the north – there's no reason to ignore one side in favor of the other, as travel between the two countries is relatively easy.

Perito Moreno is one of the few advancing glaciers to be found on the planet and regularly carves tower-block-sized chunks of impossibly blue ice into the lake

On the Chilean side, the jewel in the crown is the much-vaunted Torres del Paine National Park. Access to the park is from the eclectic little town of Puerto Natales, with its bright jumble of corrugated-tin-roofed houses, set on the edge of Last Hope Sound. Although there are roads to Puerto Natales, a more exciting way to travel is by ship from Puerto Montt, to the north. The four-day voyage skirts past Chiloé Island, where Darwin stopped during his voyage on HMS *Beagle*, and threads its way down through the Chilean Inside Passage, a mazy network of beautiful remote islands. The voyage allows you to see otherwise

inaccessible parts of the coast, where glaciers tumble from the mainland mountains into the sea, and whales, dolphins, and seals play in the freezing water.

Torres del Paine is often deemed to be the world's most spectacular national park and it is easy to see why. With its spiked granite ranges soaring from the pampas, vast glacial lakes, and outstanding hiking trails, it is unlikely to disappoint even the most well-travelled visitors. If the thought of hiking gives you cold feet, then you can always explore the park by horse or mountain bike or simply take boat trips on the lakes.

The most popular trail for more adventurous hikers, and one of the world's greatest walks is The Circuit. In six or seven days it takes you around the entire Cuernos del Paine massif, through rich green beech forests, past iceberg-strewn lakes and over high passes with views across the crevasse-scarred Southern Patagonian Ice Field that will stop you in your tracks. This is the largest ice field on the planet outside the polar regions.

Wildlife abounds in the park, with guanacos, eagles and even pumas all making their home here – though you would be extremely fortunate to glimpse a puma. Anyone who decides to camp should ensure an extra strong pitch for their tents because the region is notorious for ferocious winds, which can whip up into a gale in an instant. These storms have a real plus side, too: as dawn beckons or dusk falls you are often treated to some of the most other-worldly cloud formations and dramatic light you will ever see.

Torres del Paine may attract all the media accolades, but those in the know rave equally, if not more so, about Argentina's equivalent, Los Glaciares National Park. With little publicity and unsurfaced access roads to make your

teeth chatter, the park was once the sole preserve of hardy explorers and the world's toughest rock climbers. Nowadays, the secret of this outstanding mountain landscape is starting to get out. At its heart are the imposing red-granite walls of Mount Fitzroy and the soaring pinnacle of Cerro Torre – notoriously difficult peaks to summit on. But you don't have to be a pumped-up rock climber to see the best parts. An extensive network of increasingly well-managed trails leads you through memorable wilderness areas of lakes, mountains, and forests, with relatively few other people to block your view. Things are changing, though, as a new surfaced road heads from El Calafate, the nearest airport town, toward the park's base village, El Chaltén. Go soon before the crowds arrive.

For those who equate long hikes in the mountains with visits to the dentist, Los Glaciares National Park has a more accessible treat, the Perito Moreno glacier.

Conveniently located 50 miles southwest of El Calafate on the Brazo Rico arm of Lago Argentino, it is one of the few advancing glaciers on the planet, and regularly carves tower-block-sized chunks of impossibly blue ice into the lake. It is barely a few short steps from the car park. For added excitement you can go for a short guided walk onto the glacier and into an ice cave where you are surrounded by the ethereal blue ancient ice. With it being a popular stop on many coach tours, it won't be a solitary wilderness experience but it is Mother Nature at her impressive best all the same.

It is hard to identify geographically where Patagonia actually starts, though most people accept that the northern gateway to the region is the stunningly beautiful Lake District, straddling the border around the towns of Temuco in Chile and San Martin de los Andes in Argentina. In contrast to the dramatic mountain landscapes and dry pampas further south,

the hills here are lush with rainforest and roll more gently, except for the snow-capped volcanoes Osorno and Villarrica, which rise majestically above the skyline. From their slopes tumble glacial rivers, making for some exciting white-water rafting, and during the winter you can don your skis and swoosh down the volcanic slopes at several ski resorts.

If the northern gateway to Patagonia is difficult to define, its southern end is starkly obvious. Narrowing to a fine point around Ushuaia and Punta Arenas, any travel further south usually involves a ship bound for Antarctica. Ushuaia, in Argentina, proudly claims to be The End of the World. Arriving on just about any day in this deceptively charming little town, with its brightly painted timber houses, will involve getting buffeted by the wind. Protected from the full might of the Southern Ocean by only the narrow Beagle Channel, the wind often feels strong enough to tear your clothes off.

In between Patagonia's impressive mountain ranges lie vast tracts of pampas, typified by scrubby, water-parched, pale grasses. These seemingly inhospitable windswept lands are home to the legendary gauchos, or cowboys, who work on the huge estancias, earning a tough living from livestock. Renowned for their impressive horsemanship, their culture is based on a quiet but deep pride in their work, a solitary lifestyle, and a limitless love of yerba mate tea. Brewed in a tiny teapot and drunk through a metal straw, the tea not only helps to calm the gauchos but also subdues hunger, helpful when faced with long days riding out across the pampas.

A group of people who also call Patagonia home is the Welsh community in Chubut Province on the Argentinean side. They arrived in 1865, seeking a place where they could lead a disappearing way of life, and followed the Chubut River inland looking for suitable land. The original villages of Gaiman and Trelew remain

centers of the modern-day community. They retain many Welsh traditions and even speak Welsh.

Long before the gauchos or the Welsh arrived, Patagonia was home to the Mapuche, the People of the Land, a fearsome tribe who were the only group in South America to repel the Spanish successfully during the sixteenth-century conquest. In what became known as the Araucanian War, they killed tens of thousands of Spanish troops before the invaders admitted defeat and the Mapuche nation was formally recognized in the 1641 Treaty of Quillin. The Mapuche were finally defeated in 1885 following a prolonged campaign by the Chilean and Argentine governments, and moves began to integrate them into modern society.

From the mountain glaciers to the pampas, and from the lakes to the people, Patagonia never lets you forget how wild it is. It is a beguiling, diverse, and vast region, and a single trip can lead to a lifetime's fascination.

Atacama Desert

Fly directly over the Atacama and you understand why there's no life on Mars. Down below, the arid landscape is the closest this planet gets to replicating those photographs brought back from Martian space missions. The desert is colored with a palette of terracotta, burnt sienna, and brown. It is red and dead, with not a tree, bush, or blade of grass in sight. The airstrip you land on is just that: a ribbon of tarmac on a gravel plain with a limp windsock and nothing else. Nothing else at all.

That's how it feels in northern Chile, home of the driest desert on Earth. Much of the Atacama lies in a wide central valley that runs north to south, parallel to the coast, bordered on the Pacific side by a low range of coastal hills and to the east by the mighty snow-capped Andes. It's an area famous for its vast quantities of Chile saltpeter or sodium nitrate. The extreme aridity helps to explain why the world's most important deposits occur in the Atacama. Sodium nitrate is more soluble in water than other materials common to the Earth's crust and is plentiful here because the climate is so dry.

Sodium nitrate – a 'white gold' – was hacked out of the ground and sold all over the world as fertilizer in the late nineteenth and early twentieth centuries. Most of the mining towns that sprang up during that time, when Chile's barren north was briefly turned into a new California, have since been abandoned. They line Ruta

> Dotted along the coastline are small pockets of vegetation that survive solely on moisture from the fog. Many of these species are so finely adapted to the fogwater that they are found nowhere else on Earth

Nacional 5, the section of the Pan-American Highway that slices its way through the Atacama. It's a spooky trail of society's cast-offs: crumbling walls and deserted streets, discarded shells of buildings, and faded signs on adobe walls. The corridor of abandonment continues for hour after hour, past town after sorry town, each rejected and left to crumble slowly in the desert heat. Today, visitors flock to the El Tatio geysers in the desert. At an altitude of 14,000ft, they steam and bubble continuously, and are the world's highest geysers.

The old mining towns, like most of today's Atacama settlements, drew water from beneath the desert surface: groundwater reserves supplied by a flow from the Andes. A few rivers run westward from these mountains, but most peter out in one of the many salt lakes that punctuate the desolate terrain. Rain almost never falls in the Atacama. The meteorological data that was gathered for the last third of the twentieth century shows the small town of Quillagua to hold the record for the driest permanently inhabited place on Earth. Its average annual precipitation is just 0.012 inches.

Salty shallow depressions, their ashen surfaces cracked into polygonal patterns by the sun, are strung out along the routes down to the coast. Beyond the rolling sand dunes, fixed in suspended animation by a crust of salt, lie extraordinarily flat, gravel-strewn plateaus that end abruptly at precipitous sand-covered slopes plunging down to an aquamarine sea. Here lies one of the secrets that explain this desiccated wilderness: a cold ocean current that runs most of the length of South America's Pacific coast. The Humboldt, or Peru current brings cold water from the Antarctic, creating a cool ocean surface that minimizes evaporation, limiting the moisture in the air that can fall as rain. Add to this effect the presence of the Andes, which effectively form a barrier to the moist air from the Amazon Basin, and you have the two main reasons why the Atacama is so dry. And it's been this way for about 10 million years. The effects continue northwards, along the coastline of Peru to southern Ecuador, making this the world's longest stretch of dry land, extending for more than 2,175 miles.

While rain almost never falls, there is another manifestation of atmospheric moisture that is more common here in the Atacama's coastal zone.

Incongruously, in the late afternoon, a blast of air from far out over the Pacific Ocean rolls in off the water, rises up the coastal hills, cools, and forms fog. Although the amount of water held is small, these fogs are both regular and frequent events. Ecologically this recurrent, if limited, supply of water is crucially important. Dotted along the coastline are small pockets of vegetation that survive solely on moisture from the fogs. These lomas plants function as terrestrial islands, sort of fog oases, separated by hyper-arid habitat where virtually no vegetation exists. Many of these species are so finely adapted to the fogwater that they are found absolutely nowhere else on Earth.

People, too, have latched onto the importance of fog as a source of much-needed water. High on the hillside overlooking the small fishing village of Chungungo, an array of huge nets on poles has been set up to catch the fog as it races in off the ocean. Droplets condense on the mesh and the water drips down into plastic troughs. The troughs act just like gutters, channelling the precious collected water down through a pipe to a reservoir located near the village below.

Parts of this desert have been inhabited for nearly 10,000 years. At a few choice spots in the coastal hills, the Chinchorro people eked out a living based on the abundant marine life fed by the Humboldt current. Archaeologists think that the Chinchorro set up their camps in lomas areas, taking advantage of the fog-dependent plants and associated animals to supplement their marine diet. Some believe that the Chinchorro people collected water where the fog droplets condensed on flat cliff faces.

The Chinchorro traded with other ancient cultures in the Andes, their commercial traffic crossing the inhospitable Atacama. The trade routes probably followed the valleys dissecting the desert. Evidence of those early highways can still be seen today in the form of huge pictures on the valley sides, drawn with carefully laid patterns of stones and perfectly preserved, thanks to millennia of near-zero rainfall. Debate continues over the meaning of the intricate designs, stick men, and animals: icons to appease their gods, or desert road signs for weary travelers? They remain enigmatic riddles in the raw, austere beauty of the world's driest desert.

Grand Canyon

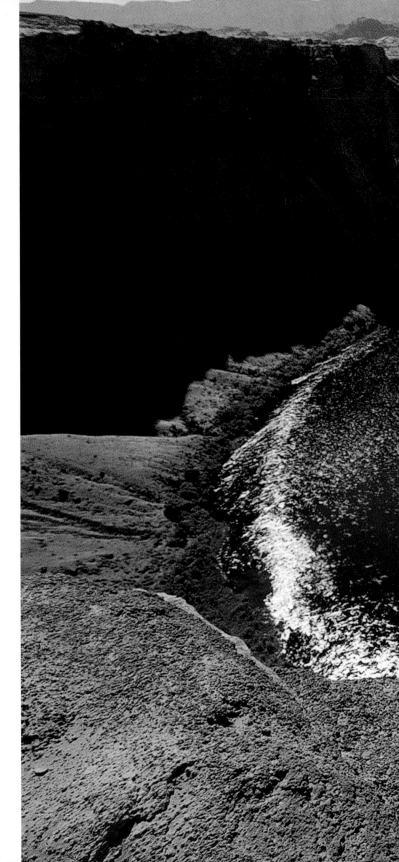

To see the Grand Canyon for the first time is to realize that it is not merely the greatest wonder on our planet, it is so overpowering that it will make you think again about the world in which you live.

Few places have the ability to overwhelm us in quite this way. It is very much an emotional response, like falling in love for the first time, and a spiritual response, too, as if gazing through the gates of heaven and hell simultaneously. More than anything, though, you feel quietly privileged to be there, lucky enough to have seen this unique place at least once in your life.

Mere statistics cannot do the Grand Canyon justice. They become almost meaningless as if the place laughs at our desire to in some way measure its outrageous scale. It covers an area of about 1.2 million acres, as if defying definition. And so it should, because no artificial units of measurement can hope to contain something that took 1.8 billion years to create. To say that the Canyon is a mile deep means nothing until you are actually standing on the edge looking down into the huge abyss, knowing that there might be someone standing on the other rim doing the very same thing as you… and they could be as far as 18 miles away from you and 1,000ft above you.

From the aptly-named Abyss viewpoint on the Rim Trail you look straight down a vertical drop of 3,000ft. That pencil-thin blue line that is sometimes visible way down at the very bottom is, in fact, the

> Mere statistics cannot do the Grand Canyon justice. They become almost meaningless as if the place laughs at our desire to in some way measure its outrageous scale

mighty Colorado River, which runs for 277 miles through the length of the Canyon and which helped to carve it out of the face of the Earth. Only helped to carve it, note, because it is only in the last six million years, a mere blip in the age of the Canyon, that the river has cut its way down through the Colorado Plateau like a saw through wood. Other factors — wind, rain, heat — have made the Canyon as wide as it is, but not even the geologists have unlocked all of its secrets.

These natural elements all play a factor in anyone's visit to this huge part of northern Arizona. From mid-October to mid-May you may not even be able to reach the less accessible North Rim, because roads are closed during bad winter weather. The South Rim, too, experiences periods of closure — winter at an elevation of 7,000ft belies Arizona's image as a desert state. Snow storms and torrential rain can bring the barriers down on the access roads at any time.

If you visit the Grand Canyon at the height of summer, though, it is a completely different picture. While temperatures on the rim reach a pleasant 80°F or so, down on the floor the Canyon becomes a cauldron, and the temperature can be a searing 100°F and more. Simply by walking down into the Canyon for an hour you pass through several different climates and 250 billion years of the Earth's history. You also seem to see 250 billion different colors in the Canyon's walls, each one telling a part of its story.

It takes twice as long to hike back up as it takes to hike down, so even a modest exploration of the Canyon requires thought. These summer months are also the wettest, and while sudden thunderstorms can turn the Canyon into a dramatic setting fit to stage a *Clash of the*

Titans, they also kill people each year. Visitors must give the Canyon the reverence it demands.

Perceptions can be false in the comfort of Grand Canyon Village, the main access point where the bulk of the Canyon's five million annual visitors fetch up. The 16-mile Rim Trail has eight shuttle-bus stops along it, making it easy for anyone to hop on the bus, stroll to the rim, take a look and a photo, and walk back to catch the next bus. Do only this and the Canyon can seem a tame place, a photo opportunity.

Walk part of the Rim Trail and the real Canyon in all its grandeur starts to open up to you. Views change slowly, as does the light. In places the trail gets very close to the Canyon's edge, and it is not a place for anyone with vertigo. The rewards are the chance to have the Canyon to yourself in places, perhaps to come across deer or sheep (hopefully not the more elusive tarantulas and snakes) or to sit quietly watching for eagles and

vultures. The extremely rare California condor, which was once almost extinct, was introduced in the Canyon area in 1996 and might be spotted soaring in the hot air currents that rise from the Canyon floor.

Some people choose to emulate the condor and soar above the Canyon by plane or helicopter from the nearby town of Tusayan, or even from Las Vegas. Because of the Canyon's physical demands, mule rides are popular, but so popular that you have to book them a year ahead. The same goes for river rafting down the Colorado. Only one of the Canyon's several trails can be completed in one day: the Grandview Trail from Grandview Point winds down over a distance of 3 miles and a descent of 2,600ft to Horseshoe Mesa. Distances are deceptive, though, and it will take an experienced hiker all day to do that round trip. Most opt to walk for a way down the Bright Angel Trail, from Grand Canyon Village, then face the hike back up again. Even this

modest adventure is more than some people in the past have achieved, such as the first Europeans to see the Canyon's majesty. These were the Spanish conquistadors, who were more interested in the Colorado River, glistening temptingly at them from the base of the Canyon. It would have slithered like a turquoise snake... and proved as elusive.

The conquistadors, under Don Garcia Lopez de Cardenas, were heading north from Mexico through Arizona, seeking the mythical Cibola, the Seven Cities of Gold. Their immediate needs, however, were more down to earth, quite literally. They needed the fresh water that they could see flowing way below them. The Grand Canyon was not about to give up this treasure to the invaders, though, a treasure worth more than gold in these lands. After four days of trying to find a path down from the Canyon's rim to the river, the conquistadors of Don Garcia Lopez de Cardenas left, still thirsting. They

were not the last to find the Canyon an unyielding barrier, coming between them and their desires.

The first Americans, other than the Native Americans, to tangle with the Grand Canyon were an army survey party. Their goal was not gold but an easier supply route to Utah. Well, perhaps it was gold of a kind: more trade. They decided, not surprisingly, that the Canyon would not provide one, and left. It was not until 1869 that the entire scale and beauty of the Canyon were fully witnessed, from down below, when John Wesley Powell made a journey down the Colorado River. His account of that trip, and the beauty he saw, was to bring the Grand Canyon to the world – and to bring the world to the Grand Canyon.

Less than 30 years after Powell's journey, showing how fast the world was changing, the Grand Canyon had gone from being unknown to being declared an American National Monument. A mere ten years later, it

became a national park. And a hundred years after that, five million people from all over the world were coming every year to gaze into the Grand Canyon.

But those five million visitors between them will never uncover some of the deepest secrets that the Canyon still clings to. Here, in the Canyon's vast lands, remains of more than 2,000 pueblos of the Anasazi people have been found. There is also the Havasu Canyon, home to the Havasupai, and on their Reservation is one of the Canyon's most beautiful settings: a lush paradise composed of thundering waterfalls and deep blue waters reached by an 8-mile hike.

The Navajo people also lived in this area, and the Hopi, too. The Hopi have a spot known as the sipapu, which only they can visit and the whereabouts of which you will not find in any book or on any map. To them, it is the hole through which they entered this world from a previous world that was destroyed.

Guilin Hills

The strange enchantment
of the limestone pinnacles
around the haunting city of
Guilin has captivated the
people and the artists of
China for thousands of years

Our Earth is alive. It breathes so slowly that we are not usually aware of it. But it moves and changes, and rebuilds itself over thousands, sometimes millions, of years. The results range from the simple beauty of the chalk cliffs at Dover in England, to the challenging majesty of the Grand Canyon in Arizona. The greatest of its creations are more than merely physical landscapes, though.

To the English, the White Cliffs of Dover represent their island home, a cliff that has repelled invaders but also welcomed returning voyagers. The Grand Canyon represents the sheer rugged immensity of the American nation. And in southern China, there is Guilin.

The strange enchantment of the limestone pinnacles around the city of Guilin has captivated the people and the artists of China for thousands of years. They describe the almost unearthly appearance of the scenery here as being the finest under heaven. The peaks evoke a feeling of mystery, as if they were somewhere between our real lives down here and another life beyond. It's as if the hills are giving us a glimpse of a heavenly landscape, visible but not yet attainable. Just like people, the mood and appearance of the Guilin Hills change with the seasons, the time of day, and the weather. Sometimes the southern China sun burns down and they stand stark against a deep blue sky, joyously grand and handsome; on other days, a river mist will roll down, hiding them behind clouds of melancholy.

Most people see the hills from the river. Even naming the river gives non-Chinese speakers difficulty, as if they are trying to pin down the flowing waters. It's known as the Gui River or the Li River or the Lijiang River, and runs for 273 miles through Guangxi Province and on into the Pearl River. For part of its length it is lined by the Guilin Hills: the section between the city of Guilin and the town of Yangshuo is the most beautiful and haunting. Small cruise boats sail between the two, floating visitors gently through the limestone peaks. What you hear as you pass through this land of enchantment are the sighs of surprise and pleasure, the 'oohs' and 'aahs' that are the same in any language.

The boat trip also provides a glimpse of life along this stretch of river, which has no more changed over the centuries than the hills themselves. It shows a people in harmony with the land around them. Children play on the riverbank, women tend tiny rice paddies, and black water buffalo peer back through green reeds. And in the middle of the river a man stands upright on his small boat, which is no more than a few lengths of thick bamboo lashed together. He poles his way upstream, a basket balanced at the rear for his catch of fish and his tethered cormorant perched in front, as if helping him look for the best fishing grounds.

These Guilin fishermen have appeared in Chinese paintings and poems over the centuries, as artists try to capture and convey the strange beauty of the Guilin Hills. The name Guilin is a little poem in itself, meaning

the 'forest of sweet osmanthus', from the osmanthus or sweet olive trees whose apricot-like scent fills the city. Several limestone hills puncture the city itself, as if they had thrust up through the Earth's crust and left the city scattered around them. Their shapes seem more regular: solid masculine mounds or more gentle feminine curves. It is along the riverbanks that the true bizarre beauty of the hills expresses itself.

The wind and rain have sculpted the soft limestone into odd shapes. Following on, man has given the shapes names — sometimes poetic, sometimes prosaic. It's the infinite variety within the similarity of the hills that is part of the charm, as if an artist had tried to show you exactly how many shades of blue he was capable of producing on the same canvas. Close to Guilin is Rooster Fighting Hill, which is actually two hills on opposite sides of the river, both resembling aggresssive roosters on the verge of a battle, forever kept apart by the peaceful flow of the water in between them. Here, too, is Elephant Trunk Hill, where nature has carved the stone into the shape of an elephant whose trunk appears to be sucking up water out of the Li River. On top of Elephant Trunk Hill is the Puxian Pagoda, built during the Ming Dynasty, and thought by some to resemble a sword sticking out of the elephant. Legend has it that the mythological elephant once started drinking the river dry. To stop it, the gods thrust a sword into the thirsty elephant.

If the elephant is distinct and solid, then Mural Hill is more ethereal. Here, Nature has produced her own artist's palette, a hundred yards high and covered in color, as if dashed and splashed on the rocky surface. The natural sculpting also extends under the peaks as it does at Crown Cave, which runs for 7.5 miles beneath the hills, adding a world of dripping water, stone, and stalactites to this land of fairytale enchantment. Legends have been caught in stone: seven hills represent the seven fairy gods who came down to Earth to bathe in the river and were so taken by the lovely landscape that they decided to stay here for ever.

The river bends and a new vista unfolds, the hills receding into the distance, all similar, yet all different — just like the people who come every day to admire them, as if hoping to catch them in the act of changing.

water

Iguassu Falls   46

Okavango Delta   50

Amazon River   56

Fjords of Norway   60

Lake Titicaca   64

Great Barrier Reef   68

River Ganges   74

Cape of Good Hope   78

Iguassu Falls

A mug of steaming cappuccino springs to mind when you encounter Iguassu Falls in full spate. There's less of the dainty, elegantly tumbling ostrich plumes of white water that you might normally associate with this Latin American beauty, and more of a roaring, frothing, coffee-colored retching that pummels your senses, leaving you damp, dazed, and slightly deaf. Swiss botanist Robert Chodat wasn't exaggerating when he described the falls as 'an ocean pouring into an abyss'.

Like all great waterfalls, Iguassu has its seasonal extremes. At the height of the rainy season, in January and February, just over 3 million gallons of water surge over the mighty series of cataracts every second. The ground trembles as spray is tossed 330ft into the air, dousing the surrounding rainforest in perpetual mist. Only Victoria Falls can match this watery exuberance – while the world-renowned Niagara Falls can manage only a comparatively weak and feeble peak flow of just 2 million gallons per second (upon seeing Iguassu, First Lady Eleanor Roosevelt reportedly exclaimed, 'Poor Niagara!')

Straddling the Brazil/Argentina border, Iguassu Falls are about 2.5 miles wide and consist of 275 cascades (between 200 and 275ft in height), separated by islands and rocky outcrops. The most spectacular is the Devil's Throat (Garganta del Diablo), a narrow horseshoe canyon where cascade and spray merge into an ethereal waterworld, like an Impressionist painting that has a life of its own.

Iguassu's cataracts beat their steady thunder; sheets of spray spurting like high-pressure steam where they strike the surface of the river

In 1541, the Spanish explorer, Álvar Núñez Cabeza de Vaca was the first European to behold the cataracts, naming them Santa Maria Falls, despite the fact that the indigenous Guaraní people referred to them as Iguazú (Great Water). According to Guaraní legend, the falls were created by Boi, a giant river snake that lurked in the Rio Iguassu. Regular human sacrifices were offered to appease the serpent, but when one intended victim, Naipú, eloped with local chief, Tarobá, the snake was so enraged that it thrashed the riverbed, carving the falls and trapping the lovers. Naipú's hair became Iguassu's cascades, while Tarobá was turned into the trees that surround the upper falls.

Mythical creatures aside, the forests surrounding Iguassu are brimming with life. Wander a few yards into this secretive, Tolkienesque world of lichen-festooned trees and shadows-within-shadows and you will soon catch fleeting glimpses of some of Iguassu's 250 species of butterflies. Some are palm-sized, gliding through the understory of ferns like psychedelic paper darts, while others are smaller, intricately patterned varieties, their multi-hued wings resembling the shards of an elaborate stained-glass window.

A hotspot of avian biodiversity, Iguassu has no less than 448 bird species, including rarities like the rufous-capped motmot, chestnut-eared aracari, and eared pygmy-tyrant. Toucans, tanagers, and parrots are the most conspicuous forest birds, although it's the turkey vultures, pirouetting overhead on finger-tipped wings, that you are most likely to notice first. Keep an eye out, too, for the red-rumped cacique, which builds hanging nests in large, rowdy treetop colonies.

Perhaps the most elusive of Iguassu's creatures are its mammals. Although some 80 species have been recorded, including the jaguar, many are nocturnal and rarely seen. There is one mammal, however, that you stand a good chance of hearing. With their guttural cries known to carry for over 3 miles, howler monkeys can make themselves heard even over the din of one of the world's greatest waterfalls.

Incredible as it may seem, even the cataracts themselves support life. If you peer closely at the spray billowing from the Devil's Throat you may well notice tiny black specks twisting and twirling like flakes of ash rising from a bonfire. These are great dusky swifts – Iguassu's iconic species. Thousands of these daring little winged wonders nest on rocky ledges behind the curtains of water (where they are safe from predators), emerging to feed on flying insects. There can be few more extreme habitats on Earth.

Considering its combination of scale, beauty, and wildlife, it is not surprising that Iguassu Falls was declared a World Heritage Site in 1984. Two national parks, one in Brazil and the other in Argentina, also help to ensure that this natural spectacle is safeguarded for future generations to enjoy. With resort hotels situated on both sides of the falls, Iguassu has established itself as a popular tourist destination. For some visitors it is enough simply to stand and gaze in awe, but as with many of the world's natural wonders, it is now possible to take part in a range of adventure activities at Iguassu that provide those who crave it with an extra burst of adrenaline.

The walking trails that go within inches of some cataracts are exciting enough, but for the ultimate viewpoint you need to get either airborne or afloat. Helicopter flights offer a wonderful, if slightly cocooned, perspective of the entire falls but, for a complete pummelling of the senses, nothing rivals a boat ride to the very base of the cataracts. Boarding an inflatable dinghy with a powerful outboard motor you approach the Great Water from a mile or so downstream.

To begin with, the falls are obscured from view as you ride a rollercoaster of rapids between cliffs dripping with subtropical vegetation. Iguassu's ominous rumbling grows louder as the boat battles its way upstream. Already soaked from cavorting through the rapids, you now begin to feel the softer, subtler touch of Iguassu's mists. Then, abruptly, you enter an arena of billowing spray where water seems to cascade from all sides. The river no longer appears to be flowing, but boiling and spurting beneath the dinghy. Cliffs and trees dissolve from view as if obscured by a sudden squall and you have a shocking, uneasy premonition of being irresistibly sucked into the Devil's Throat. Suddenly, you wince from the crushing weight of water as the dinghy noses into one of the smaller cataracts. It is a brief, terrifying, but totally exhilarating brush with Iguassu – an extreme way to experience an extreme display of nature.

Okavango Delta

Fanning out like fingers on an outstretched hand into northwest Botswana, the Okavango Delta is a lush maze of shallow channels and low-lying islands of tall grasses, palms, and acacia trees. Covering around 4,000 square miles, it is one of the world's largest inland deltas and one of Africa's greatest wildlife sanctuaries. You will find all of the big game animals here, including elephants, lions, leopards, buffalo, rhinos, and hippos, most in plentiful numbers. It is unspoilt by development or overbearing tourism, which allows for a genuine back-to-nature experience.

It is possible to find yourself at the leading edge of the Okavango flood as the water apologetically inches its way through the grasses with all the eagerness of a sloth

The Okavango River receives its source waters from the Cubango River system in the Angolan Highlands far to the northwest. It is usually December when the seasonal, subtropical rainstorms reach their peak in the mountains. Following a rapid initial descent from the highlands, the flood water slows considerably as it makes a relatively short journey across Namibia's Kavango tribal lands. By the time it enters northwest Botswana and the delta panhandle around two months later, it has slowed to a barely perceptible creep. From the panhandle to Maun, the main regional town at the delta's southeast edge, is around 40 miles, yet the flood water can take a leisurely four months to cover that distance, thanks to the shallow gradient. Defying common perception of how a flood behaves, it is possible to find yourself at the leading edge of the Okavango flood as the water apologetically

inches its way through the grasses with the eagerness of a sloth. This slow pace also causes about 98 per cent of the river water to evaporate en route.

Unlike most rivers, which eventually make their way out to sea, the Okavango River simply grinds to a halt in the Kalahari Desert, providing irrigation for much of the Kalahari Basin. Millions of years ago, when Africa formed part of the super-continent, Gondwanaland, the river flowed into the immense Lake Makgadikgadi. Geological upheaval, which created the Great African Rift Valley, then blocked off the river's route to the lake and diverted it into the delta. Because there are very few people living along its upper reaches, the river water is surprisingly pure, even when it reaches the delta, a thousand miles into its journey.

Exploring the delta is easy enough. Maun is the principal access town: from there, it is possible to fly or drive into one of the many wilderness safari camps for trips by boat, on foot, or even on horseback. Taking at least one flight is the only way to grasp the daunting extent of the delta. The Moremi Game Reserve, created in 1963 by the Batawana tribe, takes up much of the northeast part of the delta and is the focus for the majority of safari activity, partly because it is fortunate enough to retain plenty of water during the dry season, ensuring an ongoing concentration of wildlife.

Whichever way you choose to travel and to wherever in the delta, the beauty of dawn and dusk light slowly warming the Okavango's long grasses and papyrus reeds and reflecting off the tranquil waters is an experience not to be missed. In the myriad shallow pools and oxbow lakes, clusters of water lilies blossom, bringing a delicate white softness to the terrain.

Dotted around the landscape are huge, pot-bellied baobab trees. Often called upside-down trees because their branches resemble tree roots, they produce leaves for only a short period of the year, which helps to minimize evaporation. The fat baobab trunks also serve to offer some of the only shade that is available in this area from the incessant midday sun.

The delta's waters act like a giant magnet for wildlife, and this is often the main attraction for visitors. Because of the extremely low human population density in the region, the animals and birdlife have been left alone to thrive in relative peace. The area has huge numbers of elephants, which wander the delta in large herds – testament to this is the shockingly hurricane-like scene of tree damage that is clearly visible from the air. You will doubtless hear them bellowing and crashing through the bush a while before you are able to get close enough to see them, and then you may be fortunate enough to

spot a baby elephant carefully dancing its way between the dangerously close clomping feet of the adults.

Grasses and reeds can reach well above head height, making it much harder to spot lions and leopards, though, on the flip side, this is excellent news for these predators, which use the camouflage to creep stealthily toward their prey. You have a better chance of spotting them during the height of the dry season, from July to October, when the animals are forced to gather at fewer available waterholes. The tall grasses add an extra twist of drama and excitement to tracking animals in the delta. Whether you are in a four-wheel drive, a boat, or on horseback, you always feel there may be something lurking in the undergrowth.

One creature you are more likely to see in the Okavango than anywhere else is the African wild dog, an increasingly rare species. There are around 800 of them in the area, almost one-fifth of the entire estimated

population in Africa. Hunting in packs, they are effective, intelligent predators but their desire to wander far and wide has led to a severe impact on their numbers from encounters with local communities, who see them as pests. There is a concerted campaign to try to save the wild dogs from extinction but with disease also affecting the falling population, the signs are not looking good.

The wetland area is also a natural haven for birds – more than 650 species have been seen here. It is quite a spectacle to cruise the lagoons and suddenly have a massive flock of cranes, sandgrouse, or ducks lift off from the long reeds. On the lower branches of waterway trees, kingfishers, with their startling iridescent green and blue feathers, study the water surface for signs of fish. The circling vultures are a reminder of just how tough an environment this really is, and if you are fortunate enough to see them with a kill, you will be shocked at how quickly they strip the carcass bare.

If the hot, humid weather tempts you to see the delta as one gigantic swimming pool, be warned that crocodiles linger here, too. Although they are not as apparent as in other parts of Africa, it's best to stick to the camp shower for cooling off. While it is highly unlikely that you will encounter any real danger in the delta, the safari camps are open affairs, so everyone – and everything – can come and go as they please. It is not unusual to awake to find elephants or baboons wandering through the camp or to see giraffe gangling past while you are eating breakfast.

There are five different ethnic groups living in the delta, including San Bushmen, the original inhabitants of southern Africa who once roamed the region as nomadic hunter-gatherers. Although the groups still speak their own languages, their culture is under continuing threat from the relentless march of modern social and political schemes and the increasing risk of

disease, especially HIV/AIDS. There are around 50,000 San Bushmen living in Botswana's remote areas, primarily settled in small villages. Several of the ecotourism projects in the delta are owned and run by the San, as they attempt the difficult balancing act of protecting the environment of their ancestors and adapting to the economics of today's society.

While the sunrise is magical, the delta is always at its most spectacular at sunset. Dust often turns the dropping sun into a glowing red fireball, a wonderful backdrop for a romantic trip out onto the lagoons in a traditional canoe, or makoro. Overhead, great flocks of cranes, neatly lined up in a V-shape, race to find an overnight resting ground, while the chatter, roars, and screeches of the nocturnal wildlife preparing to resume their search for food fill the air. The Okavango Delta may well be as close as we can come to experiencing the planet and its wildlife in its most natural state.

Amazon River

Like the tentacles of some enormous sea creature, the Amazon and its 15,000 tributaries, many more than 1,000 miles long, are spread over eight different countries. In the snow-capped Peruvian Andes, west of Lake Titicaca, a glacial trickle next to a goat trail signifies the furthest extent of its reach. This stream flows and grows, until 116 days later it has crossed the entire continent to reach Belém on the Atlantic coast of Brazil. By this time, the river has drained nearly half of South America, and disgorges eight trillion gallons of muddy, sweet water from its mouth into the ocean every day. Here too, the river deposits the tons of silt it has collected along the way, forming Marajo – a land mass the size of Switzerland, and the world's biggest river island.

The Amazon is a monster: mythical, murderous, yet also benevolent. The word 'river' hardly does justice to this heaving, breathing juggernaut

Yet this is just one of the progeny spawned by the mother of all record breakers. The arapaima – the largest freshwater fish on the planet and three times the weight of a heavyweight boxer – makes its home here, as does the biggest snake in the world, the anaconda. As long as a killer whale, this prehistoric river-dweller swallows human victims whole and gives birth to foot-long 'babies', 50 at a time. Up above, unlucky howler monkeys are plucked from the green canopy by the ferocious harpy eagle, the king of American raptors, with a 6ft wingspan and claws like a grizzly bear.

Nor are the plants here any less spectacular. On once-in-a-lifetime Amazon river cruises, awestruck children 'walk on water' supported

by lilies twice the size of a dustbin lid, but a thousand times more beautiful. Within half a square mile, it is not unusual for nature lovers on guided treks to encounter more than 100 species of tree. The river gives life to the rainforest that surrounds it, home to five million plant species and counting.

In a shrinking natural world, Amazonia, as large as the US, is a Noah's ark for the new millennium, the natural habitat of a fifth of the world's birds, and shelter for more fish species than the Atlantic Ocean. It is also home to around 800 species of mammals, though visitors will only ever see a fraction of that total; most lurk deep in the impenetrable jungle or hide in the murky depths of the river. Yet just set foot into the rainforest and you will suddenly be surrounded by seemingly every one of its two and a half million different insects, in a buzzing, biting, and stinging frenzy. These 'pests' are a critical part of a food chain that supports the most diverse ecosystem on the planet, without which we would probably all be dead.

The 'River Sea' has the proportions of an ocean. It is 300 feet deep in parts, allowing cargo ships from the Far East and Caribbean cruise liners to steam all the way up to Manaus, 900 miles upriver from Belém. During the wet season the area of the river triples, and over the course of its journey its girth swells from one to 35 miles, making it the widest river in the world. Because it shrinks and grows according to the seasons, the river's length is hard to fathom, like the legendary Nile – with which it competes for the title of the world's longest watercourse.

After several days of sailing deep into the jungle, the hypnotic, repetitive rhythms of the river produce a dream-like state. Dramatic, multicolored sunsets come and go, and endless hours pass without seeing another boat, settlement or human activity of any kind. The Amazon swallows you whole. There is no bridge across it, and it can prove fatal to swim in it. Schools of piranha patrol the depths and locals tell tales of loved ones who went to wash by the banks, only to have their face removed in a matter of seconds.

The Amazon is a monster: mythical, murderous, yet also benevolent at times. The word river hardly does justice to this heaving, breathing juggernaut. Remote,

exotic, frightening in places, its fate is tied to our own. The Amazon produces 20 per cent of the world's oxygen and 30 per cent of the world's fresh water. As the aquatic and forest plants convert sunlight into oxygen, water evaporates, is returned to the atmosphere, and falls as rain. Without the Amazon to drive this cycle, extreme drought would ensue, and global warming would soon drive sea levels even higher, polluting what fresh water we do have. It is often said that water is the new oil, and in the future, wars may yet be fought over it.

At present, the biggest battle is simply to preserve the forest and the majestic river that nourishes it. Less than two per cent of the plant species that thrive here are properly understood by scientists; it could be that cures for many diseases may be hidden deep in the jungle. Despite this, each day an area the size of Manhattan is cleared for logging and ranching, oil exploration and road construction. In the few seconds it takes to read this sentence another city block has been felled.

Europeans settlers and their descendants have tried to bend the rainforest to their will, believing that man can accomplish anything. But trying to tame Amazonia is folly; for the first time in its history, the wettest area on the planet is experiencing drought, with river vessels stranded in the mud and dead fish rotting in the hot sun. In contrast, the indigenous people of Amazonia respect their mother river and nurture her as she nurtures them. Five thousand years of experimentation and inherited knowledge have taught them how to live in harmony with their environment. The forest provides them with all the food and medicines they could ever need. The river is their home, their highway, their pharmacy, their larder, even their god.

But as this precious habitat disappears, so do the tribes which make it their home. When the Europeans arrived around 500 years ago, there were close to six million indigenous people living in Amazonia; now there are little more than a hundred thousand. The settlers scoffed at the idea of a river god, but now science has taught us that if the Amazon leaves us, we will die. This wondrous waterway really does have the power of life and death, a supreme being, just as the Indians were told by their forefathers.

Fjords of Norway

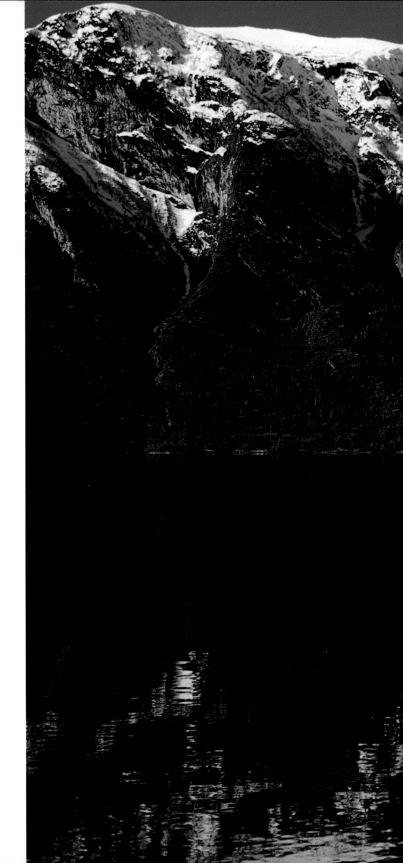

It's not always easy to get away from it all, even when you travel to the extreme ends of the Earth. At the northernmost tip of mainland Europe, a man in a Hawaiian shirt is having his picture taken with a reindeer on a lead. Dozens of cruise-ship passengers are trying on Lapp hats and waiting, cameras at the ready, for their turn with the reindeer and the North Cape Monument.

The west coast of Norway is vast, stretching over 1,865 miles from Stavanger to Nordkapp as the crow flies and an estimated 15,535 miles if you wind your string around all the twiddly bits. It is one of the great scenic destinations of the world – and wins lots of awards to prove it. The Western Fjords have been declared a UNESCO World Heritage Site; the Atlantic Road and Trollstigen (Troll's Ladder) were voted one of *The Guardian's* best road trips in the world; National Geographic Traveler readers voted them the world's greatest destination. According to Douglas Adams, writer of cult classic *The Hitchhiker's Guide to the Galaxy,* fjord-designer extraordinaire Slartibartfarst even won an award for his original frilly creation when he built the planet as a supercomputer for intergalactic white mice. This magical coast, that appears different at the turn of every season and in every change of light, deserves each one of these accolades, even if the actual designer – several hundred million tons of groaning ice – is no longer around to receive them.

Work on the masterpiece began about 25 million years ago, at the start of the last Ice Age, as slowly moving ice rivers and sheet glaciers hundreds of feet thick creaked their way off the mountains

Work on the masterpiece began about 25 million years ago, at the start of the last Ice Age, as slowly moving ice rivers and sheet glaciers hundreds of feet thick creaked their way off the mountains and out to sea, gouging out lines as vivid as earthquake scars in the bare rocks and grinding out deep narrow valleys between sheer winding walls as they went. When the ice eventually melted, around 12,000 years ago, it left the fjords – thousands of feet deeper than the Atlantic, their walls of granite and sandstone, gneiss, slate and marble battle-scarred, barricaded by mountains and the last of the glaciers from the land, their entrances guarded by a lacework of low islands from the sea. The landscape is beautiful when seen from the water and from the shore, but to be appreciated at its finest, the complex patterning of rock and water really needs to be viewed from above – perhaps it really was designed with space travelers in mind.

In the past, the fjords proved both a blessing and a curse for their inhabitants, the steep valleys providing refuge from the fierce Atlantic storms and the bitter snows that whistled across the high plateaus. Viking villagers sheltered deep at their hearts, making their livelihoods from farming the terraced slopes and fishing, venturing far out to sea in summer, trading and raiding, in search of kinder climates and gentler gradients. But where they sheltered, the fjords also imprisoned. The Vikings became superb seamen by necessity. Boats were the only realistic way to contact your nearest neighbors in the next fjord, never mind the rest of the world.

As time went on, trading cities such as Stavanger, Bergen, Tromsö, and Trondheim – grew up along the coast. All the while, the Norse Men spread out across the world from north America to Baghdad, stopped in their tracks only when the Black Death killed two-thirds of Norway's population in 1350. The survivors retreated back into the fjords, only Bergen joining the Hanseatic League and continuing to trade across the Baltic Sea. Today the west coast towns are all dwarfed by the mountains that surround them, their vibrant red, green, and blue painted houses a shout of defiance to the vastness of the elements.

Getting around the fjords isn't difficult any more. There's a train along the high ground a short distance inland, and spectacular mountain railways at Flåm and Andalsnes corkscrew down to the water's edge. Roads incorporating endless tunnels and hairpin bends wind up and down the mountains offering breathtaking panoramic views and breathtaking terror on every turn. Caravans of cruise ships crawl along the fjords all summer long and the *Hurtigruten* (coastal express), the government-run ferry, trawls up and down the coast, popping into every little settlement.

There are hundreds of fjords and every one is different. Huge Sognefjorden pierces its way inland for nearly 120 miles, its impossibly deep green waters fed by the Jostedalsbreen glacier, the largest glacier in mainland Europe, covering 188 square miles. This magical Narnia-like playground of sculpted ice, frozen waterfalls, and cloudy turquoise lakes is a hub for hiking and ice-climbing in summer, while glacier skiing takes place under a dim 24-hour dusk in winter.

Broad Hardangerfjord, itself 60 miles long, is fed by several small fingers of fjord, its placid still waters and small villages overlooked by the vast Hardangervidda plateau. Arctic foxes and snowy owls hunt their prey on this bleak ancient landscape that dates back to a time when Norway was below the Equator and this rockscape lay at the bottom of the ocean. With no tree in sight, herds of wild reindeer graze on the scrub and lichen that cling to the rocks, while trout grow plump in the icy waters of the mountain lakes. By contrast, Geirangerfjord is tiny, at only 10 miles long, and so narrow that you can almost touch the waterfalls that cascade down its rocky shores as you ease your way past. Geiranger town seems like a child's toy when seen from the summit of Dalsnibba, some 4,600ft straight above. The 25-mile long Lysefjord, near Stavanger, is lined for much of the way by layers of sheer rock, culminating in the famous flat-topped 1,850ft Pulpit Rock.

Back in the far north, it is nearly midnight and in summer it is still light enough to take photographs and still warm enough to wear the Hawaiian shirt. But in winter above the Arctic Circle it is an eerie time of almost perpetual darkness, where the gloom is broken and every chill forgotten as the sky dances into life with wave after wave of beautiful green and pink, gold and violet Northern Lights.

Lake Titicaca

On a windswept fall afternoon at the harborside on the island of Amantini on Lake Titicaca, a group of giggling local girls in traditional dress was waiting as our boat arrived. With a mix of Spanish, Quechua (the regional indigenous tongue), and bashful smiles, they led us one by one off along the island trails to meet our host family for the night.

Legend has it that, when the Spanish conquistadors ransacked the Inca wealth of the region, defiant locals threw their treasures into the lake rather than let them fall into the hands of the marauders

Here, in the Peruvian territories of Lake Titicaca, a typical family in a rural area survives on three Nuevo Soles (about $1) a day. More than 50 per cent of Peru's 28 million population lives below the poverty line. But people are happy with their lot. Life may be extreme here, but as the girls danced along the dirt tracks and through the cultivated fields of maize, corn, and potatoes, there was nothing but smiles and giggles from them.

Lake Titicaca was the jewel in the crown of the Inca Empire, a sacred place of worship and mysticism straddling the Peruvian-Bolivian border at an altitude of 12,532ft above sea level. Located at the heart of Andean South America, the lake feels both huge and remote: it covers a vast area of 3,300 square miles in the high-altitude Altiplano and is the largest lake in South America.

Legend has it that, when the Spanish conquistadors ransacked the Inca wealth of the region, defiant locals threw their treasures into the lake rather than let them fall into the hands of the marauders.

Some people believe that the mythical lost city of Atlantis may lie beneath the lake's still, deep blue waters. The French scuba diver and deep-sea explorer Jacques Cousteau even came here in search of Atlantis. He went away with not much more than a large collection of local frogs to show for his trouble.

Lake Titicaca is home to a slew of indigenous communities that are descended directly from the Inca themselves. Puno is the gateway to the lake and the port of embarkation for the majority of boat trips on the Peruvian side. Although a fairly small town it has some decent hotels and connections for internal flights arriving at nearby Juliaca airport. It also makes an excellent base in which to get acclimatized to the altitude, which can hit some people harder than a left hook from a prize fighter. The best advice is simply to rest up for a day or two and drink lots of coca-leaf tea. This has, after all, helped the locals for centuries.

From Puno, it's time to get out on the water and start island hopping. Keep an eye on the horizon – you can spot Andean condors in the skies and llamas on land while your boat chugs out into the stillness of the lake. Most tours make a stop at the floating islands of Uros, which are constructed exclusively from buoyant totora reeds. About 300 families live on the islands and rely on the reeds for almost their entire existence, using them to build their homes as well as their fishing boats.

The Quechua-speaking community of Taquile is renowned for the distinctive brightly colored, hand-woven clothes that are produced by the families on the island. Life here remains defiantly untouched by the passing of time – electricity was only introduced in 1990. There is a strong sense of cultural identity on the long and narrow island, with the proud and shy people keen to maintain their artisan traditions in the face of increasing numbers of visitors.

On the Bolivian side of Titicaca, the maritime traffic is lighter (except for the Bolivian navy, which sails on the lake since Bolivia is now landlocked), and the chance to get off the beaten track becomes far greater. The main hub is Copacabana, located at the water's edge and the primary border crossing into Peru. From here, boat trips head out to the mainly Aymara-speaking communities of the Isla del Sol and Isla de la Luna.

The former is home to the sacred rock labyrinth of Chincana. Here, according to legend, the Sun God, Viracocha, brought his son, Manco Capac, and his daughter, Mama Ocllo, the Adam and Eve of the Inca civilization, up from the depths of Lake Titicaca to found the Inca race. Inca mythology blesses the lake as the focal point for all worship to Pachamama, the Mother Earth; the mysticism and spirituality of the area can be seen in the countless ruins and traditional communities that occupy these islands.

For the ultimate insight into the traditions and mysticism of Lake Titicaca, head for the island of Amantini on the Peruvian side of the lake, where there are no phones, no internet connection, and no worries. Instead, there's just a series of Inca-style cultivated terraces rising to the skyline, a carpet of stars when the sun goes down, and a hamlet of indigenous families who are eager to welcome you into their simple island homes for the night.

That evening, after a meal of soup and rice, we went dancing. We arrived at the local village hall – a grim concrete building lit by a single halogen lamp – to find a scene reminiscent of a high-school dance: girls in all their finery on one side and awkward-looking boys in ponchos supping beers on the other. But as soon as the band struck up the first chord and the panpipes kicked in, we were all up on our feet, sashaying our way around the concrete dancefloor to the music of the Andes, with the lake ever present in the background.

Great Barrier Reef

As a cosmic phenomenon, it is in a league with the aurora borealis, or Saturn's rings: we believe in their existence, but not until we have experienced them can we have any idea of their bewitching reality. As the Space Shuttle astronauts have testified, the Great Barrier Reef (GBR) is the only collective living organism that is visible from a low Earth orbit. However, far from being a single, unified structure, the GBR is an intricate matrix made up of billions of tiny live coral polyps that, in turn, comprise about 2,500 individual reefs and 900 cays, atolls, and islands. In all, the reef accounts for about a fifth of all the coral under the ocean, and extends for more than 1,400 miles along the edge of Australia's continental shelf: from Fraser Island off the coast of Central Queensland, and up past Cape York toward the warm equatorial waters off New Guinea.

> As you get nearer, the individual reefs appear as turquoise jewels, and you see that each 'island' comprises multitudes of shallow lagoons bordered by strings of coral, like scribbles on a giant blue palette

You get a fabulous view from a helicopter. Whirring out over the cobalt Pacific in a bubble of glass is exhilarating enough in itself, but the reason for taking to the air is more than for a quick-fix thrill. Rather, it is to get a measure of the Great Barrier Reef. Soon you glimpse iridescent ribbons of reef, sparkling on the horizon between 10 and 40 miles off the Queensland coast. Then you make out lines of white foam along the outer edges, and dark canyons in between. As you get nearer, the individual reefs appear as turquoise jewels, and

you see that each 'island' comprises multitudes of shallow lagoons bordered by strings of coral, like scribbles on a giant blue palette. They come in myriad sizes, and lavish and unbelievable shapes – some freakishly extravagant, such as the immense Heart Reef off the Whitsunday Islands, so perfectly formed that it might have been designed as a godlike romantic gesture to eclipse the Taj Mahal.

If the pilot suddenly banks and the chopper lurches down toward a speck in the ocean, it is probably because he has spotted a whale. Sightings – particularly of humpbacks migrating from Antarctica between June and September – are frequent, though from an aircraft the most you see is a tiny disappearing tail that leaves a white dot on the ocean surface. Travel out to the reef by sea and there is a good chance that these leviathans will approach the boat, blast their spouts high into the air, then surface, dive, and sink into the depths, leaving

behind a flat fluke print, fizzing with spume. If you are very lucky, one will launch itself out of the water in sideways leaps, a practice known as breaching. Encounters with minke and sperm whales are also frequent, while a trip out to the reef is likely to be accompanied by dolphins arching out of the water.

When the tide recedes, the reefs are so shallow that coral appears above the surface and the sea sluices through little bays and channels between sharp peaks. This was the 'impenetrable barrier' that explorer Captain James Cook recorded when his ship the *Endeavour* became 'stuck and stuck fast' in June 1770. He finally broke free after taking measures to lighten the ship as much as possible, but had he not done so the history of Australia might have turned out very differently. In 1791 HMS *Pandora* ran aground on the reef, killing 35 people. The *Pandora* has since become one of the reef's most famous shipwrecks, and The Queensland Museum

has been organizing archaeological dig parties out to the *Pandora* since the early 1980s.

As it is, the GBR is the planet's largest protected marine park and a World Heritage Area. It is also one of Australia's most valuable sources of tourism, visited by more than two million people each year. Of these, the great majority are either on day trips from Queensland's coastal towns, or they are staying on live-aboard boats to snorkel and dive amid the coral. While the aerial view of the reef is one of Nature's visual masterpieces, it is only a meager foretaste of the awaiting underwater sensory feast. Even from the comfort of a glass-bottomed boat, the sheer mind-blowing absurdity of this vast wonderland will both inspire and shock. The kaleidoscope of color and activity, the unearthly fronds of coral swaying to and fro, the psychedelic creatures most people never knew existed, all shimmying through a mesmerizing marine habitat.

Those who don masks and fins or full scuba gear find themselves gliding through water so clear it is like a glass paperweight embedded with shells and multi-colored pebbles. This is a world of infinite richness, beauty, and complexity, where one moment you are in the midst of an explosion of striped clownfish, the next you are ogling yellow-ribbon sweetlips that pout like harlots of the deep. Larger fry, too, are commonplace; it is not unusual to swim within touching distance of a hulking, half-ton Maori wrasse, with enormous blue-green lips and a huge hump on its head. These terrifying-looking creatures are as gentle as they are inquisitive. More elusive are the giant turtles, usually greens or hawksbills, that glide mysteriously past. In all, there are at least 2,800 species of fish, 4,000 different molluscs, 15 different types of sea snake and 400 different types of coral.

A great deal of energy goes in to making tourism an ecologically sound proposition at the GBR. As one of the largest protected marine areas in the world, with approximately two million visitors each year, human activity has to be carefully controlled. In the past, overfishing has caused key damage.

At a few places, anchored pontoons float at the reef edge, where a daily quota of tourists arrive by air or high-speed catamaran, to snorkel, scuba dive, and take rides along the reef in submersible craft and watch the underwater world through the plate glass of its viewing chamber. For a truly singular experience, it is possible for small groups to overnight on a raft, floating on a tiny dot on the immense Great Barrier Reef, disconnected from the rest of the world. You lie, in the total absence of artificial light, gazing at the Southern Cross amid an astonishing profusion of stars: tiny grains of light so fine they look like luminous vapor; beaming planets; and the silky veil of the Milky Way. Then you float off to sleep, listening to the surf rippling over the coral.

River Ganges

Our self-appointed guide beckons us 'this way to the ghats' with that infuriating and captivating shake of the head that means yes, no, and maybe in universal India-speak. He points us in the direction he thinks we want to go. 'Everything helping,' he beams. Now we know we've arrived in India. It's teeming with people, it's noisy, dirty, crowded, and it's alive. There is nowhere like this country for the 'all human life is here' experience, and the silver thread that binds it all together is the River Ganges.

Ganga Ma, they call it – Mother Ganges. To every devout Hindu, it's more than their life and soul – it's their future existence. To bathe in the Ganges is to wash away everything bad from the past, and be cleansed for everything good for the future. Drinking the holy waters will ensure good health – although to the average Westerner, with an eye to what has been deposited in the river during its 1,500-mile course downstream, that seems a debatable claim. A sample of the water carried away in anything from the tiny, sealed copper vials available from any riverside bazaar to enormous plastic jerrycans, seems a prudent good luck charm for many an Indian to take home.

The Ganges flows down from an ice cave above Gangotri high in the Himalaya, down through Haridwar and on to the great North Indian plain. There it winds its way east to the giant delta that forms about half of Bangladesh. Just before it crosses out of India, the Hooghly branches off to take some of its holy waters down through

> To bathe in the Ganges is to wash away everything bad from the past, and be cleansed for everything good for the future

ladies keep their modesty more or less intact with some nifty sari-shifting beneath bamboo umbrellas. Head massages and ritual head shaving to leave just a tuft of hair at the back keep scores of barbers, expertly wielding their cut-throat razor, busy along the ghats.

On their emergence from the water, the men take great care applying the ritual tikas, or forehead markings, with make-up boxes of colored dyes and hand-held mirrors, while the women shake their wet saris out along the steps in a flurry of colors. Mingling with the 'ordinary' pilgrims are the sadhus. India's holy men are unmistakable with their bright orange robes, long matted hair, and unkempt beards, carrying aloft trident staffs and the begging bowls that are their livelihood. They jostle for space with snake charmers, who draw huge crowds. Further along the ghats, Brahmins gather in clusters to perform *puja* – intricate rituals involving spices, flowers, rice, and a great deal of chanting to ease their predecessors' journey to salvation. At dusk, the water reflects a thousand pinpricks of light, as candles are placed on banyan-leaf vessels and launched onto the river, carrying their symbolic smoke to the skies.

The magic of the Ganges is not just about life but equally about death. Hindus the world over die safe in the knowledge that their ashes will eventually be cast into Ganga Ma. The truly fortunate come to Varanasi to breathe their last because it just about assures them vacant possession of a place in their heaven. And, of course, they consign their bodies to the river in spectacular fashion: funeral processions led by chanting and trumpet-playing relatives practically queue up to get to the 'burning ghat'. Here, the bodies, shrouded in red, white, or gold cloth, are laid on pyres to be publicly cremated. The pyres are built of sandalwood for the rich, logs of banyan tree for the less well-off – boatloads of wood are delivered daily to the timber wallahs.

The aromatic smoke mingles with the mist rising from the river to create a haze that gives an ethereal quality to the buildings along the banks. Through the mist a boat comes into view, overloaded with more than 50 Indian women, saris streaming, being rowed slowly upstream. The sound of their clapping and singing is truly joyous. And so it should be. They are on Ganga Ma, the holiest river of them all. What more could they wish for?

the great teeming city of Kolkata (or Calcutta, as it was known in the glory days of the Raj). Along its course, the Ganges passes through the states of Uttar Pradesh, Bihar, and West Bengal, and in the process draws every devout Hindu to its shores. At Allahabad, there's a brisk business in boats to the Sangam, the triple confluence of the Ganges with the River Yumana, which flows from the Taj Mahal at Agra, and the mythical Sarasvati river. On the way to the Sangam, pushy boatmen surround you, selling coconuts and marigolds to scatter where the rivers meet. Because of the sacred significance of the confluence, Allahabad hosts the biggest and the best of the great Kumbh Melas, the huge gatherings that draw up to 10 million devotees, sadhus and ascetics, and which rotate around four locations every three years.

It is at Varanasi, the holiest of holy cities, on the Indian lowland roughly halfway between Delhi and Kolkata, that the River Ganges really comes into its own. All good Hindus try to visit Varanasi (formerly known as Benares) at least once in their lives to undertake ancient ceremonies that will elevate them a few rungs higher on the karma ladder, in their quest for the ultimate state of salvation that will finally free them from the cycle of reincarnation. Varanasi's daily trade is pilgrims. Immersion in the river is an essential part of the ritual, and dawn is the most auspicious time to do it. Thousands of devout Indians, young and old, gather as the sun rises over the far bank. Elderly men carefully fold threadbare garments before they descend into the water, while matronly

Cape of Good Hope

Two feathery plumes rose like white exclamation marks above the vast cobalt canvas of the ocean. They were visible for barely a second before the stiff southerly breeze seized and shredded them, but even from a cliff-top vantage point 300ft above sea level there was no mistaking the breath of two southern right whales. Mother and calf were moving slowly northward, a riveting sight made all the more thrilling by the name of the legendary headland the leviathans were rounding – the Cape of Good Hope.

The southernmost tip of the peninsula that protrudes from South Africa like a gnarled toe taking a tentative dip in the southern Atlantic, the region is hardly remote (you can drive there from Cape Town in an hour or two), but it is still a wild place of wave-gnawed cliffs, kelp-strewn beaches, and enigmatic wildlife. There may be higher sea cliffs or more rugged headlands elsewhere in the world, but few seascapes can conjure the same brooding sense of grandeur, austerity, and extreme solitude.

Looking down from the old lighthouse (built in 1860 but later moved because it was too often obscured by fog), you can't help but imagine the countless shipwrecks that lie concealed beneath the filigree of surf. Look south and your mind grapples with the fact that Antarctica is the next landfall, far beyond the horizon. Or simply gaze out to sea and contemplate the rollcall of seafaring historical giants who regarded this stub of land as the pivotal point in their pioneering world-conquering voyages.

> Look south and your mind grapples with the fact that Antarctica is the next landfall, far beyond the horizon

The first European to reach the Cape was Portuguese navigator Bartholomew Dias, who was blown here by accident during a gale in 1488. Perhaps not surprisingly he named it Cabo das Tormentas (Cape of Storms). This was later changed to Cabo da Boa Esperança (Cape of Good Hope) when its significance dawned on those plying the great East Indies trade route – if you rounded the Cape, you could hope to make good sailing to the spice islands of the Moluccas.

The seventeenth-century British explorer Sir Francis Drake famously dubbed the Cape 'The fairest… in the whole circumference of the Earth'. Other seafarers were less enamoured. Legend has it that, in 1680, the Flying Dutchman was condemned to Davy Jones's locker during a storm off the Cape of Good Hope because its captain, Hendrick van der Decken, swore a blasphemous oath. The ghost ship is said to sail whenever a gale hurls itself at the Cape. Visit during a real howler, when salt spray stings your eyes and quivering gobs of sea spume are diced against the rocks, and you begin to imagine all sorts of things, even phantom ships.

But don't see this as a desolate promontory, a sterile graveyard devoid of life. In spring you'll find ostrich and zebra stepping through lush drifts of flowers. Protected as part of Table Mountain National Park, the Cape of Good Hope is a refuge for the region's unique fynbos – a diverse floral habitat that has evolved in this far-flung corner of Africa and nowhere else. Its name means fine bush in Afrikaans, a reference to the narrow needle-like leaves of many of its shrubland species. Of the 1,100 plant species found at the Cape (including 25 proteas, 39 ericas, and 52 orchids), no less than 14 are endemic.

Mingling with the zebra and ostrich are bontebok, eland, red hartebeest, springbok, and grysbok. Not the Serengeti-sized herds you might associate with Africa, but an intriguing cast nonetheless – particularly when you happen upon a peacefully browsing group set against the surreal backdrop of an azure sea.

Perhaps the most famous Cape inhabitants are its 300 or so chacma baboons. Having learnt to associate tourists with food (thanks to thoughtless handouts, which are now forbidden), these intelligent, powerful and occasionally aggressive primates have developed something of a notorious image. However, give them

the respect (and distance) they deserve and you might be lucky enough to observe a troop doing what baboons do best – foraging for food. The Cape's baboons are particularly adept at this, supplementing their normal diet of bulbs, grass seeds, and insects with a seafood course of limpets and crustaceans.

Beachcombing can also be a rewarding pastime for humans on the peninsula. The strandlines on beaches like Buffelsbaai are often drizzled with prizes such as cuttlefish bones, sea urchins, mermaids' purses and other interesting treasures of the tide.

Whereas the nutrient-poor fynbos can sustain only a limited number of land animals, there is no such restriction on life in the seas around the Cape of Good Hope. Two great ocean currents – the cold Benguela and warm Agulhas – converge in these waters, infusing them with nutrients to create a rich pelagic broth that is the lifeblood of the Cape's teeming seas. Beachcombing provides tantalizing evidence of this fecundity, while the 3,000-strong colony of African penguins at Boulders Beach near Simon's Town leaves you in little doubt as to the region's extraordinary marine wealth.

However, it is only when you venture beyond the shore that you fully appreciate the biodiversity of the seas that swirl around the Cape of Good Hope. A marine protected area was declared in 2004 to safeguard species ranging from abalone and rock lobster to cape salmon and bottlenose dolphin. Two ocean dwellers epitomize the wildness of the Cape more than any other. One is the Cape fur seal, which forms crowded colonies on islands in False Bay and further along the coast towards Cape Agulhas, and the other is the Great White shark, which has feeding, not breeding, on its mind. Great Whites are frequently seen breaching during their ferocious assaults on the seals.

The seas surrounding South Africa's celebrated headland may well be the best place on Earth to witness these magnificent predators in action but, ultimately, the essence of the Cape of Good Hope has more to do with extreme contrasts than extreme carnivores. It is a place where the life-giving seas are littered with shipwrecks, where baboons dine on oysters, and where the calmness of a warm spring day can be shattered by an icy gale, born and bred in the Southern Ocean.

fire

Mount Etna   84

Namib Desert   88

Sahara Desert   94

Yellowstone Geysers   98

Volcanoes National Park   102

Australian Outback   106

Death Valley   112

Krakatoa   116

Mount Etna

It holds the world record for eruptions, is Europe's largest and most active volcano, and has been called the greatest pyrotechnic show on Earth. And yet this fire-breathing dragon, capable of destroying everything in its wake, is loved and deeply respected by the locals. Ask any mountain guide why *il vulcano* – masculine in Italian – is called 'she' and the reply comes: 'Etna is dangerous and mysterious, just like a beautiful woman.' La Signora Etna is hero-worshipped; people make offerings and bless their houses to escape her wrath. Even when she is at her most sultry and smoldering, wiping out all obstacles in her path, hapless homeowners, forced to abandon their dwellings, leave bread, cheese, and wine to satisfy and appease her. Even gods of destruction need rest and food.

The first rumblings began around 1500BC. The Sicels, original inhabitants of Sicily, worshipped Adranus, the fire god, who was said to live under the volcano before being driven out by the Greek god Vulcan, who made it into his subterranean forge. His groans, creaks, and hammerings accounted for the violent, earth-shaking eruptions, echoing the Greek word 'Etna', meaning 'I burn'. Today, it is Europe's highest volcano – literally a highlight of any trip to Sicily – towering at 11,155ft with a perimeter of 155 miles.

The huge, black graceful cone of Mount Etna is visible all over the island. In the words of Goethe, 'the whole panorama is capped by the huge, fuming, fiery mountain, the look of which, tempered by

> Unlike its murderous cousin, Vesuvius, Etna's rivers of lava tend to move slowly down its flanks, giving people a chance to escape

distance and atmosphere, is, however, more friendly than forbidding'. Unlike its murderous cousin Vesuvius, Etna's rivers of lava tend to move slowly down its flanks, giving people a chance to escape. According to Etna expert Boris Behncke of the nearby University of Catania, in its entire recorded history, only 73 confirmed deaths have been directly attributed to eruptions. And on several occasions the veil of Sicily's patron saint, St Agatha, has been used to confront the fury, and stem the lava flow as if by a miracle.

Yet the explosive potential has, until recently, been underestimated. The major eruptions in 2001 and 2002–2003 showed that Etna is more than capable of significant activity, with strong earthquakes and fountains of lava spewing from cones and craters. The sounds of unearthly creaks and murmurs echoed from far below, accompanied by a flurry of molten volcanic bombs flying through the air. Seas of lava cascaded downhill, sweeping through the middle of the mountain hut at Rifugio Sapienza, attacking the cable car that ran to the top, engulfing three of its pylons and melting its cables. Etna pumped so much ash and red-hot molten rock into the sky that it eventually forced the closure of Catania airport, 16 miles away.

Bocca Nuova, 'the new mouth', is – as its name suggests – the youngest of Etna's craters, all of which are active, and has recently eclipsed the others in a spectacular show of power and heat in November 2006. Showers of glowing lava were accompanied by a number of fiery explosions – lapilli of molten rocks. Strombolian fountains erupted literally every second, reaching up to 600ft high. Snow melted in a trice with the air temperatures quickly soaring from 23°F to more than 104°F, and ribbons of steam hissed their way through the funnelling wind.

Yet 20 per cent of the population of Sicily lives around Catania and Mongibello – the Sicilian name for this mountain of mountains. The foothills of Etna are densely wooded with oaks, poplars, chestnuts, beech, and birch – an artist's palette splashed with vibrant yellow broom, the flame red of the briar rose, and fiery hues of the spurge. The contrast between the green Mediterranean sheen of the vegetation and slick black of the lava moonscape is dramatic.

Lava, when hardened, is the perfect environment for plants. The fertile volcanic ash has made the land ideal for producing sun-drenched fruits; there are silvery olive groves, orchards, nut plantations, and luscious vineyards. Mount Etna is also the site of the world's biggest horse chestnut tree – the Castagno dei Cento Cavalli – a staggering 92ft high and 170ft in circumference, and more than 2,000 years old.

Clinging to the mountain's flanks are dark volcanic villages, such as the ski resort of Linguaglossa – a corruption of *lingua grossa,* meaning fat tongue. The tongues of black lava that engulfed the village in 2001 are still visible on the south face on the way up from Nicolosi to the Rifugio Sapienza. That eruption poured out of a side cone, bursting open just a few hundred yards from the tourist shops, burying the ski facilities and almost engulfing the main square of the resort of Piano Provenzana.

On a good day, with no volcanic activity, guided excursions by off-road vehicles and on foot to the summit leave from Piano Provenzana at 5,940ft. En route to the craters, you pass seas of lava from the 2002 eruption. The tendrils of now cold lava that poured down into the stretches of pine forest, lacerating the green mantle and revealing centuries-old trees burnt like twigs, are an eerily heartstopping sight.

From the top, glorious vistas of the crystal blue waters of the Ionian Sea, fringed by a halo of golden sands unfold. Far below are vineyards, citrus, and oak groves. Forest gives way to lava fields turned to stone. Underfoot, the tortured shapes of the hot, rugged terrain that has been buffeted in turn by the wind, thin air, and sulphuric fumes make the going at times treacherous. But the infernal vision of the three peak-top craters concealing the fiery red and yellow molten river is completely unforgettable.

The apocalyptic fireworks of this fire mountain continue to fascinate, terrify, and bewitch. Locals point out that she was here 200 million years ago and that we should never speak badly of her and should try to satisfy her every whim. To guests on her slopes, she is both friend and enemy, giver and taker. Mere mortals have always been insignificant in the face of this eternally unpredictable, smoldering beauty.

Namib Desert

A sea of swirling sand is whipped by scorching desert winds; colors shimmer, fade and glow. In the vast emptiness of the Namib Desert the world's highest sand dunes rise majestically from the Sossusvlei valley floor, big, bold, and blazing an unforgettably deep orange that burns itself onto the back of your mind like a laser. This is a landscape constantly changing, blown into shape by arid sand-shifting winds. These persistently refine the dunes, sculpting knife-edge arêtes, sweeping simple distinct folds, forming and reforming the spectacular steep-sided cliffs.

In the vast emptiness of the Namib Desert the world's highest sand dunes rise majestically from the Sossusvlei valley floor, big, bold and blazing an unforgettably deep orange

The dunes make you want to climb them. At 980ft, Dune 7 is the highest but Dune 45 is by far the most accessible. Even so, each step along its razor-sharp ridge is an effort. The initial sensation of warm, soft, delicate sand, spilling between your toes, quickly gives way to the dragging heaviness of each foothold. You don't walk, you trudge, and every step feels like a mini sand-slide. But you won't stop. In the Nama language namib means vast. At Sossusvlei, 186 miles from any main highway, scaling one of these dunes – sandblasted and tired – you get a true sense of what the word vast really means.

Namibia is an immense country, more than triple the size of Great Britain. The Sossusvlei dunes are part of the 19,300-square-mile Namib-Naukluft Park, which is one of the largest conservation areas in the world. Covered for the most part by rich swathes of

ochre sand, swept from the Kalahari five million years ago, the mysterious Namib Desert is believed to be the oldest desert in the world.

Not only can you find the highest and oldest dunes, but you can also discover ones that make a noise: the roaring dunes. Strapped into a four-wheel drive, carefully perched on the lip of what feels distinctly like a sand cliff, can be a stomach-churning moment. The handbrake is released and slowly, serenely, you drop over the edge. Almost immediately the noise starts: a low steady hum. Specifically sized particles of sand create this unique audible reaction to any friction, to the point you'd almost swear there was a World War II bomber overhead. This unique and bizarre phenomenon exists only in the dunes found further north, accessed from Terrace Bay.

The roaring dunes are part of a bleakly named area known as the Skeleton Coast. Here a narrow strip of wilderness separates the Namib Desert from Africa's

loneliest and most savage coastline, a maritime graveyard for unwary ships. It's a meeting point, where the icy waters of the Atlantic clash with the warm desert air, causing a notoriously disorientating sea fog that wraps and clings to anything in its path. It's an evocative, haunting place – the curse of sailors for centuries – and unpredictable currents and sandbanks have served to make it both famed and feared.

Taking to the skies in a small light aircraft gives you an immense perspective on the vast loneliness of this seaboard. There is nothing, just an endless stretch of pristine beaches. But look carefully and you will see the occasional hardy hyena feeding on the remains of the coast's latest victim. The sight of many shipwrecks, boats keeled over in the sand, rusting in their sandy graves, is a truly powerful reminder of the savagery it can inflict.

The *Eduard Bohlen* is one of the most famous, a steamer that ran aground at Conception Bay in 1909. Its

corroding hull lies partially buried and now several yards inland from the shore, a sign that the desert is slowly creeping westward to the sea, reclaiming the land.

Touching down on a rough landing strip to explore this empty landscape is eerily beguiling. At the remains of an abandoned mining operation, books lie scattered on the floor of a dilapidated shed: their pages flicker in the wind, a corrugated-iron roof creaks. For a moment it's almost as if you can hear the voices of past inhabitants, the whirring chime of machinery, but then the swirling desert winds come and the moment is lost. Outside, whale bones can be found among polished surf-lashed pebbles, and the lure of diamonds makes for the ultimate beachcombing. Further on, the sound of more than a million basking sea lions delivering a cacophony of coughing, wheezing splutters while huddled lazily on the wave-pounded shoreline is unmistakable. They look like a soft furry patchwork of grays and browns. Situated 62 miles north of Swakopmund, the Cape Cross Colony is the largest in Southern Africa, where the sea lions fight, sleep, swim and smell — and eat 550 tons of fish a day.

Flying inland from here you can explore a lunar landscape of brooding black ridges where the Kalahari and Congo plates collided. Here the force of tectonic activity has created a ripple of rock formations. The dark presence of the Ugab Formations makes a stark contrast with the white of the desert. If you touch down in the nearby Huab Valley, an expanse of red and yellow sandstone, the surrounding hills hold another sign of ancient activity. Nestled in the sides of the rock are the caves of the San bushmen who once tracked here. If you look closely, you can find their rock drawings.

Not so easy to spot are Namibia's prized desert elephants, found in the northwestern region of the Namib known as Damaraland. In this dry and arid landscape the search for water is constant. Hiding out at a watering hole, you wait for them to appear. Finally, sedately emerging from the bush, the elephants travel as a group. Mothers shield their young, in perfect step with each other, like a slow swaying train. Each footfall is placed with a mesmerizing rhythmic quality.

With baking heat and soaring temperatures, this can be a punishing place to live. In the northern Skeleton Coast, in Kaokoland, the Himba people cover themselves in an ochre paste as protection from the sun; they are Namibia's only remaining nomadic tribe. Living in small adobe huts, they continue to eke out an existence.

Namibia is a bold and uncompromising landscape, harsh in its remoteness and beautiful for its cosmos of color and contour. Its dunes roar, rumble, smoke, and move as though a living part of the landscape. You can get the sand out of your hair. Getting it out of your system may not be quite so easy.

Sahara Desert

A land of broiling sun, blistering winds, and endlessly shifting sands, the Sahara Desert is probably the most inhospitable region on the planet. Even the Tuareg tribes, who have 'tamed' it as well as anyone ever could, have learned to treat it with great respect and are ever on the alert for the first signs of its treachery.

> You question everything in the Sahara and you quickly learn not to trust your eyes. Nothing can ever be taken for granted here, and a sensible visitor must try to gauge conditions with the mind of a sailor

In remote nomad camps and kasbahs there are countless tales of experienced desert pilgrims who were nevertheless tricked into a wrong turn by a landscape that seems to shift and warp before your eyes. Even a relatively small change in the wind can transform an entire dune range, creating a maze in which the most cautious of wayfarers will become irretrievably lost. All too often their desiccated corpses are found where they slipped into their last parched sleep on the leeward side of a dune.

Rusted cars lie like the husks of giant beetles all over the edge of Sahara, and as you drive past – concentrating on every variation in the hum of your engine, scanning the sandy floor for hidden rocks – you take each one as a reminder of the awareness and preparation needed to travel in the world's largest desert. As you weave through the rolling dunes of Western Sahara, you learn to keep one eye on the compass and another on that blazing sun. Drift too far east and you could end up lost in a wilderness of rock and sand in which there is nothing of substance before you reach the Nile valley 3,000 miles away.

Even on a relatively short visit it becomes apparent that there is really nowhere like the Sahara – with its inconceivable size and sheer emptiness – for instilling a respect for the world's most extreme places. Touching on 10 separate countries and stretching the width of North Africa, the Sahara is a surprisingly varied region. Very little is actually covered by the rolling dunes of *Lawrence of Arabia* fame. Much of it is rocky hamada plains, speckled with hardy scrub and ribbed with dry, sandy river-courses. Known as wadis, or oueds, these rivers might run with water only once in a lifetime.

By night the desert is a far more benign place. After the fiery heat of the day, the coolness of evening is a blessing. You wrap up cosily in a blanket or djellaba cloak and boost the camp fire. Out in the shadows a couple of hungry jackals start up an eery whine at the aroma of sizzling barbecued lamb. The stars, unmolested by anything more than a few street lamps for hundreds of miles, cover you in a great glittering dome that seems to rest directly on the horizon. Seen through the clarity of the desert atmosphere, the heavens are a busy place, with shooting stars and satellites always on the move. Early morning, too, is clear and crisp, and the heavy dew that falls in the night can often be a surprise to newcomers to the desert. But as the piercing sun climbs higher, all moisture quickly evaporates… and the Sahara returns to its old tricky ways.

You must question everything in the desert and you quickly learn not to trust your eyes. You struggle to convince yourself that the shimmering lake that you can make out quite clearly on the horizon is only a mirage. The camel herders know that what looks to be a relatively lush pasture – intensified by the endless expanses of a desert plain – will turn out to be nothing but a few sparse clumps of spiky grass when they finally arrive. Yet, in this harshest of environments, they also know that this is about all they can expect. They give thanks to Allah for small blessings.

A shadow gathers on the horizon and you strain your eyes as a dusty frontier town begins to spread its skirt toward you. The desert towns could almost be natural creations of the Sahara itself in the way that they reflect the gold or ochre of the surrounding land. From a distance they often appear only as a ragged dune. You get the sense that your perception of them is deepened by the obstinate vitality that pulses beneath their shells.

Occasionally you see camels moving across an otherwise empty, lizard-baking desert, their legs melted into a watery mirage so that they seem to sail like true ships of the desert. In this boundless desolation you wonder where they have been and where they are heading for so doggedly. More importantly, you wonder whether they will ever get there. Nothing is taken for granted here, and a sensible visitor must try to gauge conditions with the mind of a sailor.

You watch the sky and try to cultivate a nomad's sensitivity for variations in the hot chergui wind. There is a great tradition of blind Saharan guides who navigate by the smell of the prevailing winds, which are far more reliable than the ever-changing dune formations. In the scale of the Sahara, though, a sandstorm can race across the landscape at a speed that even the Tuaregs find hard to anticipate. If you are lucky enough to be in a village or a nomad camp, the first sign you are likely to have of a sandstorm is the sudden fleeing to shelter of all the people around you. Peering through a door or a tent flap, you see it arrive: a coffee-colored wall, over 300ft high. It tears across the peaceful landscape, shredding and scattering everything it touches. It slams doors and shakes tents like an angry djinn, or poltergeist. It hits you like a blast from an oven door. The sand blisters and pelts you, and you duck under cover and pray the tent will hold together. If you are in a vehicle, you grip the steering wheel and hope the storm will cease before the wheels get buried. As you sit there waiting, the ubiquitous tales of lost caravans and buried armies suddenly do not seem so far-fetched.

It's possible for a serious sandstorm to last many hours – or even, in some areas, days – but the desert people simply wait it out with unshakeable patience. Generations of lives in this inhospitable and unpredictable wilderness have taught them to accept their fate (known here as baraka) with good grace. When it is over, they emerge to fix their roofs, bolster their ravaged date palms, and clear ancient irrigation ditches. Sandstorms like this are no more than minor inconveniences – whims of the djinn – for people who dare to carve a living out of the Sahara.

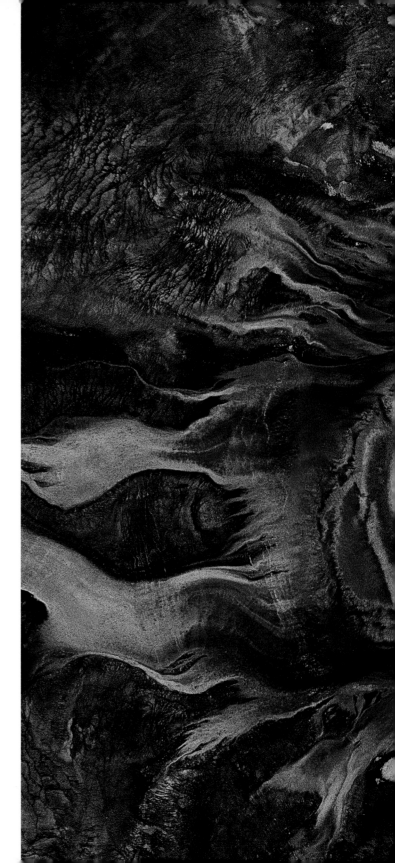

Yellowstone Geysers

With its awesome geothermal phenomena, formed by the largest volcanic system on the continent, Yellowstone was once thought to be 'the place where hell bubbles up'

Deep inside the ground, it begins. Water from rain and snow, trickling down through the porous earth, reaches a layer of molten rock some two miles below the surface. Heated to well above boiling point, the water expands into a pressurized mass of steam, forced upward through cracks and fissures, seeking escape. It finally breaks through a crusty, cone-shaped hole in the ground, and as the first splashes and small jets emerge, a ripple of excitement runs through the gathering crowd.

They have come to see the world's most famous geyser, Old Faithful, put on its show in Yellowstone National Park. They are never disappointed. Within minutes, one of these jets becomes a full-blown eruption, spouting a fountain of boiling water and steam to heights of 106-184ft – higher than Niagara Falls. Up to 8,400 gallons of water are expelled during eruptions, which last from 1.5 to 5 minutes. They happen, on average, every 91 minutes.

Despite its name, Old Faithful is neither the most regular nor the biggest geyser in Yellowstone. The park contains more than 300 of them, two-thirds of all the geysers on Earth. They lie in a series of basins, many of which are centered around the aptly named Firehole River. Like powerful and mysterious elemental spirits, each has a form and personality of its own. Whirligig Geyser spins in its crater while it sprays. Grand Geyser erupts in thrusting bursts that soar above the nearby trees, while Fountain Geyser blasts out wildly

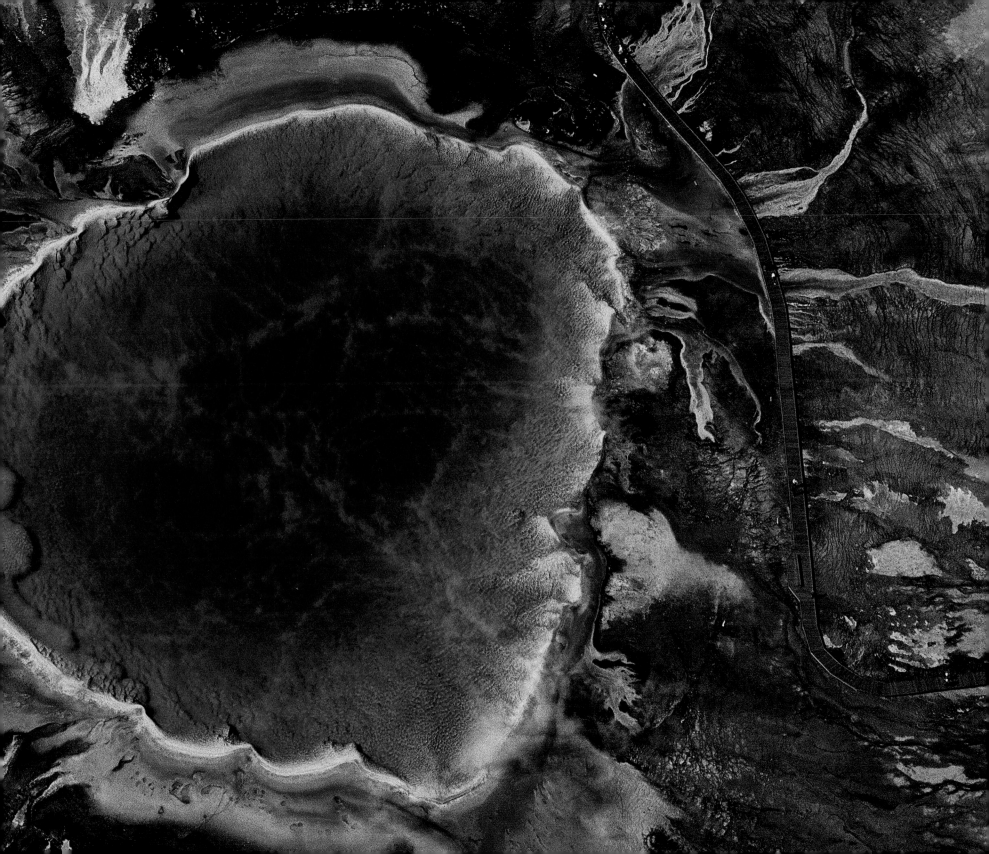

in all directions. Riverside Geyser creates misty rainbows as it spurts at an angle over the river. Some erupt as frequently as every 30 minutes. Others, like Steamboat, the world's tallest geyser, which reaches heights of 300-400ft, can take years between eruptions. With its amazing geothermal phenomena, formed by the largest volcanic system on the continent, Yellowstone was thought to be 'the place where hell bubbles up'.

Half of all the hydrothermal features in the world are found in Yellowstone, numbering more than 10,000. Along with the geysers, there are steaming fumaroles, bubbling mudpots, and pool after pool of sizzling hot springs edged in a supernatural palette of colors. To walk amid this primeval landscape is to imagine what the Earth must have looked like when it was first formed.

Although these sights are more evocative of the depths of Hades, Yellowstone in fact occupies a high plateau in the Rocky Mountains. It covers more than 2.2 million acres in northwestern Wyoming, spilling over into Montana and Idaho. Most of it lies above 7,500ft in altitude. The Continental Divide snakes diagonally across the southern portion of the park, with many of the geothermal features occurring nearby. Surrounding them are the flora and fauna that comprise some of the most pristine wilderness in North America.

In the early 1800s, fur trappers and explorers were the first white men to see Yellowstone. They reported fantastic sightings of waterfalls gushing upward and lakes of boiling mud. Their stories of fire and brimstone in the geyser basins were quickly dismissed as tall tales. But later expeditions led to the preservation of this unique wonderland, and the designation of Yellowstone in 1872 as the world's first national park.

Yellowstone's scenery is so captivating, its vistas so grand, its aura so peaceful, that it's easy to forget its violent origins. This land was formed by volcanic activity over millions of years, leading up to the cataclysmic explosion of a supervolcano 640,000 years ago. The volume of ash spewed out by this massive eruption – which was 450 times greater than that of Mount St Helens in 1980 – covered all of the western states, much of the Midwest, and northern Mexico. It left behind the Yellowstone Caldera, measuring 30 miles wide, 45 miles long, and thousands of feet deep.

Over the centuries, much of the crater was filled in by lava flows. Yellowstone Lake takes up the rest. But beneath it all, the volcano is still active. Between 1,000 and 3,000 earthquakes are recorded here every year. And this same hotspot provides the searing temperatures that fuel the park's hydrothermal features.

These pockets of Yellowstone often appear harsh and raw, like the landscape of some far-off moon. As it bubbles to the surface, the boiling water carries with it particles from the bowels of the earth, particularly silica, the mineral used to make glass. Above ground, it forms a rock called geyserite, or sinter, which creates the bizarre scenery of the geyser basins, from the colossal geyser cones and scalloped crusts around the hot springs to the milky frosting on the flat expanse of Porcelain Basin. In some spots, the noxious fumes of sulphur and other geothermal gases, occasionally toxic, are a reminder of nature's terrible subterranean power.

Yellowstone's thermal areas are fascinating and strangely beautiful. Minerals and microorganisms paint surreal colors across this stark canvas, from lime-green algae to orange deposits of iron oxide. Yellow sulphur deposits combine with deep-water blue to form the Emerald Spring. The brilliantly hued Grand Prismatic Spring, with rings of red, orange, yellow, and green surrounding its bright blue center, is created by mats of bacteria growing in the warm, mineral-laden water.

Some of the most curious features, despite their rotten-egg smell, are the bubbling mudpots, formed when sulphuric acid dissolves silica and clay into shallow thermal waters. Fumaroles are literally steam vents, found on hillsides and higher ground, where the superheated water boils away before reaching the surface, expelling only hissing gases and steam.

Elsewhere, hot water flowing through deposits of limestone has created the massive travertine terraces of Mammoth Hot Springs. The park's volcanic origins are clearly seen in the dramatic Grand Canyon of the Yellowstone. Here, the Yellowstone River carves a deep gorge through layer upon layer of ancient lava flows, revealing the yellow-hued rock that gave the park its name. Far underground, the volcano seethes. It will erupt again, maybe in the next 10 years, maybe in the next 10,000. Meanwhile, Old Faithful marks time.

Volcanoes National Park

Flaming fountains of molten rock cast an eerie orange glow against the night sky. Red-hot lava bubbles through the Earth's crust and becomes a river of fire, creeping across the blackened terrain, scorching everything in its path, twisting and hardening into an alien landscape. At the base of the mountain it pours over stark cliffs into the sea, sending up billowing clouds of toxic gases.

While it may look more like the backdrop to a fantasy film, this is the dramatic face of Hawaii Volcanoes National Park. Located on the eastern side of the Big Island of Hawaii, 30 miles southwest of the town of Hilo, this World Heritage Site is unlike any other national park in North America. Here you can walk across two of the world's most active volcanoes, Kilauea and Mauna Loa, and observe the volcanic forces that have been at work for some 70 million years.

Established in 1916, the park covers 333,000 acres and is still expanding. Lava flowing from Kilauea created 600 new acres in less than two decades. The ongoing eruptions in the volcano's East Rift Zone began in 1983, the longest series in recorded history. While the blue hulk of Mauna Loa, which last erupted in 1984, slumbers peacefully in the park's western quarter, everyone is aware that it could awaken at any moment. Every week, more than 1,200 earthquakes are measured on the island.

When you watch the volcanic action in the park, you are catching a glimpse of the birth of the Hawaiian Islands. This archipelago,

> Temperatures are extreme – around 2,000°F at the point of eruption. The lava has to flow for around 20 miles before it begins to cool and harden

which encompasses eight large islands and 124 smaller islands and atolls, spreads across 1,640 miles of the central Pacific Ocean. More than 2,000 miles from the nearest continent, it is some of the most isolated terrain on the planet, a place of balmy temperatures and lush foliage created by fierce eruptions on the ocean floor.

These islands and their volcanoes are made of billions of tons of magma, built up over many millennia. When measured from its base on the sea bed, Mauna Loa rises to 56,000ft, nearly twice the height of Everest. Covering 19,000 cubic miles, it is the most massive mountain on Earth. Layer upon layer, Mauna Loa has grown by about 300 acres each century. A similar process is taking place some 20 miles south of Big Island, where another offshore volcano more than 3,000ft deep is slowly creating a new Hawaiian island from the ocean floor. Already named Loihi, it should reach the surface in about 10,000 years.

History's most famous volcanoes have erupted violently, blasting lava and ash into the air for miles around through steep cone-shaped summits. But Hawaii's volcanoes are known as shield, or fissure, volcanoes. Instead of the volatile gases that cause such explosions, they have a regular flow of magma, or molten rock, to the surface. Hotter and more fluid, it produces fire fountains and slow-moving trails of molten lava that leave rounded mountains in their wake. The origin of this river of fire lies 50 miles beneath the surface, where pools of magma in the Earth's mantle are moved upward by currents of heat to a reservoir beneath the volcano. As pressure builds, magma is forced through fissures in the Earth's crust, eventually bursting through the volcano's summit or along a rift zone.

Hawaii has two types of lava flows. Aa (pronounced 'ah-ah') lava, also known as scoria, forms crusty lava fields of angular, twisted chunks, often sharp as glass. Pahoehoe ('pa-hoy-hoy') is more liquid and forms a thin, smooth skin as it hardens, often wrinkling into lava beds like piles of coiled rope. Its surface is thick enough to walk on, but hot lava continues to flow in a tunnel underneath.

The park encompasses an amazing variety of terrain, from tropical beaches of black volcanic sand to snowfields on Mauna Loa's summit. In between is an otherworldly landscape of craters, cinder cones, steam vents, pumice heaps, and vast lava fields up to 3 miles wide, dotted with islands of vegetation. Winding through it are 140 miles of hiking trails.

On the northern and eastern slopes of Kilauea, rainfall can exceed 150 inches a year, producing a lush rainforest of fan palms, tree ferns, and ohi'a trees with bright red blooms. By contrast, on the dry southwestern slopes, lava areas such as the Ka'u Desert are almost barren.

The park contains an impressive range of endemic flora and fauna, which evolved from organisms carried to the emerging islands on trade winds, sea currents, and on the wings of birds. Many non-native species that were introduced by humans now threaten the ecological balance, but the park preserves endangered species such as the nene, or Hawaiian goose, the hawksbill turtle – one of the archipelago's few large native animals – and the Hawaiian honeycreeper, a finch-like bird.

Wide calderas crown the summits of both of the park's volcanoes. Crater Rim Drive, an 11-mile road that circles Kilauea's 4,000ft summit, gives access to strange volcanic phenomena such as Sulphur Banks, where fluorescent yellow steam vents give off gases reeking of rotten eggs, and the tunnel-like Thurston Lava Tube, high enough to walk through. The Chain of Craters Road descends the slopes of the volcano, where you can often watch active lava flows.

In such a fantastical environment, it's easy to believe the ancient Hawaiian legends of Pele, goddess of the volcano, who makes her home in the Halema'uma'u crater at the summit of Kilauea. Called 'the woman who devours the land', she hurls fire, melts rocks, and builds mountains and islands. To appease her, people still leave ceremonial offerings at the edge of the crater. Liquid lava that is blown through the air into thin strands of volcanic glass is known as Pele's hair.

The Hawaiian islands were first settled by Polynesians more than 1,600 years ago. The early Hawaiians etched tens of thousands of petroglyphs in the hardened lava of Pu'uloa, and left fossilized footprints in the Ka'u Desert ash. By and large they learned to live with Pele's violent tantrums, though as recently as 1990 lava buried the village of Kalapana. Today, instead of running away, people flock to see Pele's fury. In Hawaii Volcanoes National Park they can enjoy the spectacle in safety.

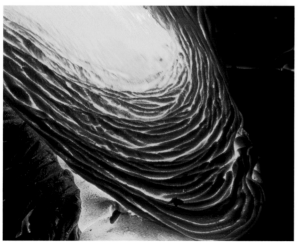

Australian Outback

In the far northwest lies the unknown Kimberley region, a magical isolated mixture of bizarre landscapes, dramatic waterfalls, and the most remote Aborigine tribes

Throw a dart at a map of Australia and the chances are it will hit the huge central expanse of scrubby desert known as the outback. To the uninitiated, travelling across this immense wilderness seems to offer nothing but an endless flat panorama of reddish earth and reddish rocks, broken only by knee-high green scrub bush covered in a thin veneer of reddish dust. Scratch beneath the surface, though, and take the time to travel more extensively and you will find the very heart of Australia. Written into the rocks and earth are stories of the aeons-old Aborigine culture; the wilderness tracks echo the relatively modern history of the first European explorers.

Australia is the largest island in the world, measuring about 2,500 miles across and 2,200 miles from north to south, and yet almost the entire population of 22 million live in a dozen or so main cities on a thin coastal fringe. So, when Australians talk about 'going bush' – their affectionate tag for the outback – there's more than a lifetime's worth of bush to explore.

Setting out on any journey into the outback needs careful consideration. Australia is the driest continent outside Antarctica and a simple mishap out in the center can quickly turn into a survival challenge due to the lack of water – let alone the enormous distances and sparse population to call on for assistance.

Without doubt, the most famous place in the outback is Uluru, also known as Ayers Rock. Set in the Uluru-Kata Tjuta National Park,

this 1,135ft sandstone rock formation rises majestically from the desert floor, dominating the landscape for miles around. Imbued with stories from the Aborigine Dreamtime – their creation period when spirit beings roamed the Earth making its natural features – the rock remains a spiritual place for the traditional Anangu landowners. No matter how many photographs of Uluru you have seen, nothing prepares you for the wonder of watching the sandstone change from burnt orange, flame red to deep purple, at sunrise and sunset.

While Uluru attracts thousands of visitors, the western area of the outback is perhaps the least travelled. In the far northwest lies the Kimberley region, a magical isolated mixture of bizarre landscapes, dramatic waterfalls, and remote Aborigine communities. It is so infrequently visited that one of its prime geological attractions, the otherworldly Purnululu, or Bungle Bungle, rock formations was only discovered by outsiders in 1982, 160 miles south of the town of Kununurra. This collection of beehive-shaped dome mountains and deep gorges has been formed by erosion over the past 20 million years. The domes are made even more striking by their stripy layers of orange, black, and gray rock. Exploring the domes and gorges leads you to a succession of Aborigine rock art sites, with paintings dating back tens of thousands of years.

With only one surfaced road in the region, getting to the Kimberley region requires going off-road. It has one of Australia's great wilderness driving tracks, the Gibb River Road. Stretching for more than 400 miles, the road runs from Derby, near the west coast, to Kununurra on the border of Northern Territory. If you don't want to camp every night, there are several homestays on old

cattle stations along the way, where you can meet some of the characters who call this wild place home. With their nearest neighbors several hours' drive away, it takes a certain type of person to make a life in the outback.

A two-day detour from the Gibb River Road leads north, through even more remote country to the Mitchell Plateau. You really are a long way from anywhere up here, but seeing the magnificent four-tiered Mitchell Falls tumble down huge steps in the plateau, makes the trip worthwhile. At night, there is nothing better than to roll out your swag – a traditional canvas sleeping bag used by stockmen – and sleep under a clear outback sky streaked with shooting stars.

Around 150 miles east of Darwin in the Northern Territory is one of the outback's wilderness gems, the World Heritage-listed Kakadu National Park. This immense flood plain, with its verdant foliage and extensive wildlife, including enormous saltwater

crocodiles, lies in stark contrast to much of the outback. It also has an array of Aborigine rock art sites, such as the galleries around Nourlangie Rock, where skeletal figures of the creator spirits and creatures mix with paintings of the cosmos and stencilled handprints left by Aborigines thousands of years ago. Around the park are a succession of lush gorges, such as Maguk Gorge with its deep, green waterhole, and several waterfalls including Jim Jim Falls, which thunders down from the high escarpment. Adjacent to Kakadu's eastern flank is Arnhem Land, a relatively unexplored region of subtropical savannah, which is becoming known for its strong Aboriginal culture and some of the oldest and most pristine rock art ever found.

The northeastern region of the outback is all within the state of Queensland. It was the setting for one of Australia's most legendary explorations, the epic and ultimately tragic 1860–61 expedition to cross the

country from south to north, led by Burke and Wills. Along with 17 other men, and many camels and horses, they pioneered a route from Melbourne to the Gulf of Carpentaria, some 1,740 miles away across punishing desert terrain. With a South Australian government reward of £2,000 up for grabs to the first successful south–north crossing, they pushed hard and successfully reached their northern goal. Then things went terribly wrong. Monsoon rains turned the route into a quagmire, plans fell apart, and disease struck. Only one man, John King, managed to return all the way to Melbourne while seven men perished, including Burke and Wills, who starved to death near Cooper's Creek. Despite their failure and errors, it is still seen as a heroic expedition.

One of the quirkiest towns in the outback is Coober Pedy, a lonely 525 miles inland from Adelaide in South Australia. Set among harsh rocky semi-desert terrain, the town is the self-proclaimed Opal Capital of the World,

thanks to its extensive networks of mines. Coober Pedy's strangeness comes from much of the town being built underground in caves. Given the extreme surface temperatures, which can soar to above 122°F during the day and plummet to freezing overnight, the natural insulation provided by the caves makes a lot of sense. Settling into your desert-cave hotel room is both weird and exciting, like having a childhood den with en suite facilities and pizza delivery just a phone call away.

If long days of tough outback driving don't appeal, the newly extended Ghan Railway is an alternative way to see a large cross-section of the landscape. Now running the entire 1,851 miles from Adelaide on the south coast, via Alice Springs to Darwin on the north coast, this luxury train ride takes just three days if you don't break the journey. As you dine on gourmet cuisine and sip fine Australian wines, though, it is worth taking a moment to ponder what Burke and Wills endured.

Among the ocean of isolation that's on offer in the outback, one of the loneliest stretches is the Nullarbor Plain, just to the south of the Great Victoria Desert in Western Australia. This is where the highway runs arrow straight for more miles than you care to count. As a passenger dozing off for a few hours, you're unlikely to wake up to a different view out of the window. It is flat scrubby desert followed by flat scrubby desert, with an occasional kangaroo to break the monotony. When a solitary roadhouse appears on the shimmering horizon, your relief at seeing a sliver of civilization is countered by astonishment that anybody would choose to live in such a remote, unforgiving place. But take time to chat to the owners and it is likely you will get a glimpse of their hardy spirit and passion for the outback's extreme landscapes. It will also help to understand how this beguiling wilderness can unlock the primordial wild spirit that lies somewhere in all of us.

Death Valley

The Salt Creek pupfish is about 2 inches long and exists in a territory roughly 1ft square, which it defends as vigorously as any creature on this earth. The entire world's population of this unique species lives in a part of Death Valley that is perhaps the size of a few football pitches. The pupfish can survive in water that is four times saltier than sea water, and can withstand the searing summer temperatures that make this part of eastern California one of the hottest places on the planet. Throw an unsuspecting salmon into Salt Creek in the summer and it would be poached to perfection in seconds, if a little over-salty.

Death still haunts parts of the landscape, seen in the skulls and bones of beasts on the barren ground. In some places even the trees have withered and died to resemble human corpses, twisted in torment

The pupfish has adapted to life in Death Valley just as the Timbisha people, part of the Shoshone tribe, did at least a thousand years ago, despite the challenges. Summer temperatures in recent years have hovered round the 134°F mark, consistently the hottest on earth: 134.7°F was recorded in Death Valley in 2001 at Furnace Creek Ranch. Only the Sahara Desert approaches it for persistent heat: 136.4°F was recorded once in Libya in 1922. In some places, the ground temperature can be up to half as hot again as the air temperature, making it one of the few places where you can literally fry an egg on the ground.

Alongside these harsh facts, though, are other more surprising ones. Death Valley also has snow-capped peaks and carpets of

that is intensified when the land is surrounded by mountains, trapping the heat generated like an oven. Only 76 miles west of here, Mount Whitney at 14,505ft is the highest point in the Lower 48 (that is, all of the states apart from Hawaii and Alaska). Little wonder that the air in thees parts gets so hot it can burn your nostrils as you breathe in and out.

The extremes are built into the very fabric of the place, in the names people have given it over the years: Badwater, Black Mountains, Dante's View, Furnace Creek. And, as ever, there are contradictions. Furnace Creek may have long held the record for being the hottest spot in North America, but these days visitors can enjoy a round of golf at Furnace Creek Ranch, the lowest course on earth, 214ft below sea level. Nearby is the natural phenomenon known as the Devil's Golf Course, a surreal surface where columns and craters of salt up to 2ft high stretch away into the distance. This gives you the unearthly feeling that you're walking on the moon, or certainly somewhere not on this planet.

It's a feeling that will become more common, because Death Valley itself might one day face death at the hands of man. Despite the creation of the National Park in 1933 and the protection this affords, mere laws on paper can do nothing about what happens deep below the ground and in the skies above. Global warming means that within the lifetime of this book, a new world record temperature will almost certainly be recorded – and almost certainly in Death Valley. Down below the earth, the complicated watering system of this part of the world (where fewer than 2 inches of rain fall a year), is being tested by growing populations in western California. Water is being drained in ever-increasing amounts and springs are slowly drying up.

The home of the Salt Creek pupfish is threatened. So, too, is that of its even rarer and smaller relative, the Devil's Hole pupfish, of which fewer than 500 survive. In fact because of seasonal fluctuations, the population of this 1-inch long creature – which lives for a year if it's lucky – drops below a hundred in the spring. As the heat continues to rise, and the waters to fall, it faces being squeezed out of existence. And it will be more than merely one more death in Death Valley. It will be something for all of us to mourn.

wildflowers. Contrary to popular belief, it didn't get its name because of the many pioneers who died while crossing the land in their eagerness to join the California Gold Rush of 1849. Those who took the Death Valley route crossed the desert in December, a pleasant time of year down on the valley floor – they were in more danger of dying from the cold in the heights of the Nevada Mountains. Only one person is known to have died en route: an elderly man, already sick from the strain of crossing the Nevada deserts before even seeing Death Valley. The deaths that gave the valley its name were those of the oxen the pioneers had to slaughter to survive. That, and an emotional response to a place that tested them physically, as it still does today, even if the traveller is in the comfort of an air-conditioned vehicle rather than a covered wagon.

Images of death still haunt the landscape, visible in the skulls and bones of beasts lying on the barren ground. In some places even the trees have withered and died to resemble twisted human corpses. Despite the snowy mountains and the alpine flowers, this is the pervading image of Death Valley. It is a land of dry sand and gaunt rock, of bare, inhospitable mountains with ragged indents like the ribs of a dead whale, of swirling dunes and a scorching furnace heat.

Death Valley is a land of extremes. Badwater is the lowest point in North America, 282ft below sea level – one reason for the boiling heat. The closer you are to the center of the earth, the hotter it becomes, an effect

Krakatoa

Despite its brooding power, the world's most famous volcano is also a place of eerie beauty; there are patches of primrose-yellow sulphur-beds and boulders still hot and bejewelled with golden crystals

Volcanoes have a way of reminding us that the ground beneath us is not to be taken for granted. 'Civilization exists by geological consent,' a wise man once wrote: 'it is subject to change without notice.' If there is one volcano that stands testament to the subterranean forces that are constantly rumbling under the thin crust of rock on which we live, it is Krakatoa.

On 27 August 1883, this almost unnoticed and uninhabited Indonesian island suddenly blasted itself to smithereens: 36,417 people were killed by the 120ft tsunami that crashed onto the coasts of nearby Java and Sumatra. The explosion was described as the loudest bang ever heard by modern man, and the sound of 'cannon-fire' was reported as far away as India and central Australia. The wave raced across the Indian Ocean at a speed of 400 miles an hour. It carried corpses to the beaches of Africa and was felt by sailors as far away as the English Channel. Eleven cubic miles of rock were shot 17 miles into the air (three times the height of Everest). The shock wave travelled the world seven times, and the dust orbited Earth to cause several summer-less years brightened only by apocalyptic sunsets.

Such inconceivable facts as these are never likely to be far from your mind on a small boat bound for the world's most notorious volcano. The Krakatoa archipelago lies just 27 miles west of Java, but the treacherous currents, fickle winds, and hungry sharks of the

Sunda Straits are good reasons for renting a reliable boat and an experienced guide. After about two hours in the company of only soaring frigate birds and darting flying fish, the huge rainforested wedge of Rakata Island rises above the horizon. Since the great mountain blew its top, this is the highest point in the islands.

In the eruption, every living thing in the archipelago was blasted out of existence, and the rioting jungle that now covers Rakata is a unique 120-year-old experiment in nature's powers of recolonization. The plants arrived as windblown rafts from the mainland. They carried snakes, lizards, rats, and the land crabs that you find even half a tortuous mile from the beach. Just 40 years after the eruption, scientists recorded 621 animals on the already forested slopes of Rakata.

The island has not often been climbed, and it can take several hours to cut a trail to the summit. But it is worth the struggle when you finally clear a 'window' in the canopy of trees and take in the view across the Sunda Straits. To the east are the volcanic hills of Java, and to the west the jungles of Sumatra. To the north you see Long Island and the rocky outcrop that seventeenth-century Dutch sailors knew as Verlaten Island (Forbidden Island). And dead ahead, across just a few hundred yards of shark-infested waters, you finally set eyes upon Krakatoa.

Menacing wisps of smoke snake toward you, and a thick smear of ash across the cone testifies to recent activity of a more violent sort. Known in Indonesia as Anak Krakatoa (son of Krakatoa), this 'smoking gun' is all that is left of the great killer mountain. In fact, Krakatoa had four 'sons' before this one. Three times since the great explosion the cone erupted over the surface of the water, only to be battered back down by the waves. Anak Krakatoa finally raised its head on 12 August 1930 and continues to grow about 20ft a year.

Unfortunately for the long-suffering inhabitants of this part of Indonesia, the constant shifting and clashing of tectonic plates is a source of devastating power that can be monitored by modern science but will never be controlled, or even predicted with any degree of certainty. Just as there are families on the coast who remember the old story of how great-grandfather survived Krakatoa, there are now many more who can tell horrendous tales of loved ones lost to more recent, tragic and even more insatiable, tsunamis.

A few intrepid Sumatran fishermen – descendants of the men who brought the first reports of boiling sea, exploding beaches, and pre-cooked fish to the incredulous Dutch authorities just before the 1883 eruption – have returned to reap the harvest of these rich thermal waters. Crossing the few hundred yards from Rakata and camping alongside them on the peaceful beach at Krakatoa, it can be an eerie sensation to recall suddenly that you are at the epicenter of one of the world's most dangerously unstable regions. Eighty years ago there was nothing but saltwater on this spot, and several eruptions in more recent years have buried the island again under thousands of tons of rubble. Even with such unsettling thoughts in your head, the gentle lapping of the waves and the balmy Asian night cast a spell that lulls you to sleep within minutes.

The best time for taking photographs on Krakatoa's summit is at sunrise when the volcano is still only visible as a triangular shadow among the incredible canopy of stars. You step through the narrow band of pioneer casuarina trees and a few stands of tough grasses and, as you start up the slope, you realize that you are trying not to wake the sleeping giant. It is tough going on the sliding scree but there are occasional volcanic slabs that offer a place to rest and catch your breath. But you are careful not to breathe too deeply. Noxious clouds swirl on the trade winds, seeming to pursue you. Your eyes are watering and your nose stings as you finally lean over the crater rim, to peer into what a Victorian writer once called 'the gates of hell'. Yet the summit of Krakatoa is also a place of eerie beauty. There are patches of primrose-yellow sulphur-beds and boulders bejewelled with golden crystals.

Just like a well-tended baby, Anak Krakatoa's every burp and gurgle are noted by watchful guardians. At Java's Krakatao Volcano Observatory the dark threats of this precocious and powerful infant are constantly being scribbled onto a seismographic print-out. According to the scientists who are on round-the-clock duty as baby-minders, the infant has been holding his breath recently and, as every attentive parent knows, this cannot last. Another gargantuan temper tantrum may be on its way.

ice

Greenland   122

Yakutia   126

Alaska   130

Baltoro Glacier   136

Iceland   140

Antarctic Peninsula   146

Lapland   150

Greenland

Greenland may be known as the world's largest island but most of its terrain is impossible to see. Four-fifths of it lies permanently buried beneath a blanket of ice that is up to 1.86 miles thick. This enormous ice sheet stretches 1,500 miles from north to south and 800 miles across, a vast, bleak, and lifeless expanse of frozen water. It contains 10 per cent of the world's fresh water, and it is second in size only to the awesome expanse of the Antarctic ice sheet.

At its edges, the ice sheet frequently dispatches portly glaciers to ooze down toward the coast like slow-motion rivers of ice-cold white lava

This icy wilderness is not a featureless desert. From the air, it resembles the rough hide of some ancient beast, cracked and textured like the skin of an elephant, a maze of crevices, fractures, and crevasses. The snow and ice can take on a thousand shapes and textures. In some areas, snow is sculptured into aerodynamic forms reminiscent of small sand dunes, all aligned on the course of predominant winds, their crests sparkling into the distance in the sunlight. Ice becomes twinkling, sugar-coated ridges and small blue pools fed by trickles of meltwater. Look in one direction and the vista is perfectly smooth, as only snow can be; in another it becomes rough and wind-hewn with elongated crystals of ice directing your gaze to some far-off vanishing point away in the distance.

At its edges, the ice sheet dispatches portly glaciers to ooze down toward the coast like slow-motion rivers of white lava. Their inexorable path gouges invisible canyons as they go, spitting out icebergs into the cobalt waters of the Atlantic Ocean. The major

glaciers of West Greenland produce, or calve, most of the icebergs that reach the North Atlantic. Where a glacier meets the ocean, these gigantic lumps of ice are weakened and finally broken off by the rising and falling motion of the tides. The newly formed icebergs are able to float because the glaciers are composed of fresh water, which is less dense than sea water.

The small town of Ilulissat stands at the snout of one of the world's most productive glaciers, a colossal conveyor belt dropping off 22 million tons of ice a day – enough to supply the whole of New York City with water for a year. Its icebergs float serenely in Ilulissat's bay, some the height of four-story buildings.

Although Greenland is the world's largest island – Australia is bigger but it is classed as a continent – its human population is only about 57,000. Most people live beyond the edges of the ice, tucked away in small remote settlements that remain unconnected by roads. Journeys between the settlements have to be made by dogsled or snowmobile when there's enough snow on the ground, otherwise travel is by air or ship.

The little hamlets become fewer and further between the farther north you go. It is no surprise to learn that the Greenland National Park is the world's largest protected area, covering 375,000 square miles – the entire northeast section of the island. Generally speaking, the further to the north, the colder, drier and less windy Greenland becomes. In the far north, winter temperatures may drop to -58°F.

A lack of sunshine helps to keep temperatures low in winter. Most of the island lies inside the Arctic Circle, that imaginary ring with the North Pole at its center, enclosing an immense area where the tilt of the Earth on its axis means that in summer the sun never sets and in winter it does not rise for days on end.

These long severe winters mean snow cover for eight months of the year and adjoining large tracts of ocean that freeze solid to several yards deep. All along the shoreline and beyond, giant icebergs become immobilized in the frozen waters, fixed in suspended animation on the petrified ocean.

The snowmelt season that begins as spring fades into the arctic summer is important for many people in Greenland, not least for the indigenous Inuit who make their living as hunters in the wild north. Northern Greenland is not suitable for any form of agriculture so hunting has always been the only means of subsistence. Seals, polar bears, walruses, and a variety of birdlife are common prey, and the prolonged days of summer open the way for extended hunting trips lasting several weeks.

From some time in June the sea ice in the far northwest begins to break up, offering a window of opportunity in which, for a few months, the hunters can pit their wits against the biggest prize that nature has to offer: a whale. International regulations allow Greenland's Inuits a small annual quota of whales to hunt. The hunting method used is simple and centuries old: a harpoon cast from a tiny kayak.

The greatest prize is a narwhal, a permanent inhabitant of these cold Arctic seas. This is the whale with the spiralling tusk that, until the early seventeenth century, was thought in Europe to be the horn of the legendary unicorn. In times past, in a land with no trees, where even a small piece of driftwood was a rare and precious commodity, its ivory tusk was invaluable. The Inuit used them as tent poles, fashioned them into arrows and harpoons, and carved them to make runners for their sleds. Even in the early twentieth century, narwhal tusks were still employed to make handles for the nets used to catch seabirds – like butterfly nets but with somewhat bigger mesh.

Today, even when wood can be imported, the tusk remains an esteemed prize with a high commercial value. The hunter whose harpoon is first to stick is the one who carries off this precious trophy. The tusk is carved into finely worked figures, jewellery, or even a walking stick and then sold. The cash received is critical to help pay the rent and buy heating oil, ammunition, and clothing at the village shop. A whale's meat provides months of food for the hunter, his family, and his dogs. The narwhal's skin is a cherished delicacy; it is rich in vitamins and tastes like hazelnuts.

When, in mid-October, the sea ice forms once again off the northernmost settlements in Greenland, it does so very fast. This marks the end of the narwhal hunting season. The endless sunshine gradually seeps away into the continuous night of winter and another year slips by on the world's largest island.

Yakutia

Deep in the heart of Siberia, in a meadow on a river, is a small town named Oymyakon. It has wooden houses and a school. Most of its inhabitants keep horses and cattle; some have a few reindeer. Oymyakon is similar to hundreds of other settlements all across the huge Siberian region of Yakutia, except for one thing: Oymyakon holds the record as the coldest permanently inhabited town on Earth. The average temperature in January is -58.2°F but the lowest temperature ever recorded here is commemorated by a monument given pride of place in the middle of town. Set in a stone base, surrounded by a low wooden fence, a model of a thermometer records the historic low of the 1920s. The temperature shown is -96.2°F.

Yakutia lies in the northeastern part of Asia, covering more than 1,150,000 square miles. It is Russia's largest region, occupying one-fifth of the country's territory, and stretching across three time zones. The climate is severely continental. Not only is it the coldest region in the northern hemisphere, but also the most seasonally extreme. The difference in temperature between the winter lows and summer highs has been known to exceed 180°F.

In winter, life in Yakutia's deep freeze comes with some curious quirks. Handling anything metal can be dangerous because touching it with bare skin causes the moisture on your skin to freeze and stick to the metal. If you pull away, you may leave a layer of skin

In especially clear and cold conditions, you may hear a strange, faint rustling sound while standing outside. This is caused by the settling of tiny ice particles from your breath

behind. In especially clear and cold conditions (-58°F and below), you may hear a strange, faint rustling sound while standing outside. This is caused by the settling of tiny ice particles from your breath. They are produced by sublimation – when water vapor freezes directly to become solid ice. It's like hearing leaves in a breeze, or grain being poured into some distant elevator. The Yakuts, one of the region's indigenous groups, call this phenomenon 'the whisper of the stars'.

For the meteorologist, severe sub-zero temperatures require special measures. Most thermometers are designed to utilize the thermal expansion of a liquid in a glass tube. Mercury, the common constituent of thermometers in more temperate climes, is no good in Yakutia because it freezes at -37.8°F, so ethyl alcohol (which freezes at -175°F) is used instead.

Traditionally, many of Yakutia's indigenous peoples have been herders and hunters. To cope with severe winters, their diet is rich in animal products, particularly meat, and they wear warm boots, coats, mittens, and hats made from animal skins and furs. The warmest fur for hats comes from sable, but pinemarten and fox are also very good and reindeer skin makes the best boots. Fur keeps animals warm because it traps air between the hairs to provide insulation. Reindeer fur is particularly efficient because each individual hair is hollow.

The inhabitants of Oymyakon may no longer roam the forests and plains, but reliance on animals is no less important than in generations past. Their Yakut horses are hardy beasts, left to forage outside for themselves through even the harshest months. They have short legs and heavy compact bodies, which means the ratio of their surface area to volume is low, helping them to preserve heat. But these horses still rely in part on human assistance. Every couple of months in the winter they are rounded up and brushed down with heavy metal combs and scrapers. Snow that collects on their backs turns to ice, both a heavy burden for the animals and an icy threat to their health.

Rivers and lakes throughout Yakutia are frozen solid for the duration of winter. Almost half of the region lies inside the Arctic Circle, and much of its territory is underlain by permafrost (ground that remains frozen to great depths throughout the year). Building cities on such icy terrain requires special measures because a heated house placed directly on permafrost can melt the surface layers, resulting in dangerous subsidence. Architects meet these challenges by preserving the earth's thermal equilibrium. Every contemporary structure in Yakutsk, Yakutia's capital, stands above the ground on concrete stilts. Pipes, too, are difficult to bury, so the urban landscape is a maze of heavily lagged pipelines winding their way all over town, feeding apartments and offices with water and removing waste.

Much of the countryside in Yakutia is seemingly endless tundra, where trees cannot grow, dominated by herbs, mosses, and lichens, favorite pastures for reindeer. Summer sunshine melts the wintry mantle of snow to reveal great carpets of green, while south of the tundra, larch, fir, and pine trees dominate the vast evergreen taiga, or boreal, forests. This is part of the world's largest swathe of forest that stretches the entire width of Russia, from the far east of Siberia through northern Finland to the Atlantic coast of Norway. Much of the taiga is marshy in the few spring and summer months, its atmosphere alive with the high-pitched buzzing of mosquitoes. Birds arrive to nest, lay their eggs, and feast on the plentiful insects. But when many of its creatures disappear for the winter, to hibernate or migrate to warmer lands, this forest takes on another guise.

Snowflakes fall and frost takes hold of the trees. The tall, narrow, pointy shape of conifers means that the snow tends to slide off their branches; their needles also shed snow more easily than broad leaves – adaptations that reduce the likelihood of heavy snow breaking branches. In the windier spots, the snowless trees can look skeletal, standing as black and dark brown silhouettes against a brilliant white prospect.

But in areas where the winds are light the scene is different. It's a wintry wonderland of quite exceptional beauty, populated by trees that look snug in their snowy winter coats. Penetrating deeper into this breathtaking landscape, the virgin snow touched only by the tracks of a deer or an arctic hare, the trees look as if they have been decorated with giant blobs of cotton wool.

Bathed in crisp, clean sunlight, this is a panorama of magic, an environment of serenity wrapped in a silence that is little short of primeval.

Alaska

The glacier's name is Ruth. It is a simple unpoetic kind of name for something that fills the deepest gorge in North America, the Great Gorge, almost 2 miles from top to bottom. And if you were to stand on the top of that gorge, then the tip of Mount McKinley, the highest point in the United States of America, would be another 3 miles above you. There are 2 miles of solid ice beneath your feet, and 3 miles of crisp, clean air above your head. Welcome to Alaska.

You are standing on a glacier, formed over millions of years and so vast that its own weight causes it to move imperceptibly, like a great, lumbering elephant

The native Aleut people called it Alyeska, the great country. Well over twice the size of Texas, and the second-largest state in the US, Alaska is a sparsely populated extreme land in the extreme northwest of the North American continent. It shakes hands with Siberia across the Bering Strait, close enough to walk. In March 2006, two explorers did just that and walked across the 56 miles of frozen sea into Russia, and were arrested for not entering the country through an official border control. Alaska is truly the end of the American earth. To hijack L P Hartley's famous phrase, 'Alaska is foreign country: they do things differently there'.

Anchorage is its largest city, bigger than the state of Rhode Island, and two-fifths of the entire population lives there: all 280,000 of them. There are just over 600,000 people in the whole state of Alaska. There are also 3.5 million lakes that are greater than 20 acres in size. Smaller than that, they stop counting. Where other

cities have car parks for their commuters, Anchorage has parking for sea planes. Thousands of sea planes, the only way for many people in these parts to get around. There are occasional problems with moose swimming across the runway, and you don't argue with a moose. They may look goofy, but they can and do kill people.

Bears kill people, too. Every country has its potentially lethal hazards, whether snakes or spiders, muggers or motor cars. In Alaska, people live with the possibility – in some areas, the probability – that they will one day encounter a bear. In fact, 98 per cent of the US's brown bears live in Alaska, perhaps as many as 45,000 of them. There are grizzlies and polar bears as well, the latter in the northern and western reaches of the state, and ideally suited to cope with the harsh climate there. So, too, are wolves: Alaska is home to around 9,000, the biggest population in the US. What attracts the wolves and the bears – remoteness from people, the food supply – is what also attracts some humans. And the locals grow up knowing about wildlife behavior, and what to do when you meet a brown bear or a grizzly.

It's easy to meet one. Even in spots popular with visitors, like the little town of McCarthy high in the Wrangell-St Elias National Park, it's not unknown for a bear to be seen walking down the main street. It can add a certain edge to a tourist's usual stroll before breakfast. In the modern manmade world in which most of us live, it's inspiring to know that places like McCarthy still exist. The road to McCarthy, dubbed the worst road in Alaska, doesn't actually get there. The dirt road that winds for 60 miles over a former railroad track (and the spikes can still surface and deflate your tyres) peters out before it reaches journey's end. It stops one side of the

Kennecott River, and McCarthy is a five-minute walk on the other side of the footbridge.

It takes a special kind of person to live in a land like this, where for many even a place like McCarthy (population 42) is too busy. Walk a few miles out of town, keeping an eye open for bears, and you'll find the homes of people who moved out here 40 or 50 years ago as settlers, who built their own homes with their own hands, in some cases even built their own planes. It's a land for individuals, for free spirits, and free thinkers. A conversation with someone who lives in a place like the Wrangell-St Elias National Park is never boring, definitely never predictable.

At 13 million acres, the park is the largest in the US – the size of six Yellowstones and bigger than West Virginia. It has just two roads – and one of those is the infamous road to McCarthy. It has the biggest concentration of glaciers in North America. It is where four major

mountain ranges meet, and where you will find nine of the 16 highest peaks in the US. It is a place of superlatives, a place where not even seeing is believing.

You have to breathe a place like Alaska to understand it. The air is crisp and clean. In winter it's more than crisp, it's so cold it can freeze your eyelashes together. So cold you can step out of a plane at Anchorage Airport and your camera freezes shut, a warning that you cannot hope to capture Alaska's beauty or reconstruct its grandeur, even in the best of photographs.

To fly over the land in a plane, large or small, is to start to appreciate the scale and the poetry. Down below, a bear lollops over the stubbly earth, her two cubs racing after her with all the cuteness of youth. Another sits by a river when the salmon spawn, watching and waiting for supper. The rivers teem with salmon, literally millions of them swimming upstream – the sockeye, the coho, the king salmon, the Copper River, and the Yukon River

salmon, which are delicacies to both man and bear. Ahead of you looms the white pyramid peak of Mount McKinley, 20,320ft high.

The native people called Mount McKinley Denali, the High One, with an understatement that speaks with respect. Denali looks down on the Great Gorge and on that glacier called Ruth, where your sightseeing plane can touch down. The snow is so smooth you fear the plane will never come to a halt, but stop it does and out you step. Your toes tingle, your cheeks too, and you breathe air like you've never breathed before. You are standing on a glacier, formed over millions of years and so vast that its own weight causes it to move imperceptibly, like a great, lumbering elephant. The whiteness is blinding, and billowing pillows of white peaks completely surround you. They hold you in the palm of their hand, like an ice King Kong, and you feel the decision is theirs as to whether you live or die.

Despite the summer sun, the blue skies and lakes, despite the periods when crops grow, when eagles breed, when bear cubs feel the first warmth of spring, Alaska is a land ruled by ice. Some 16,000 square miles of its surface, about the size of New Hampshire and New Jersey combined, are covered by glacial ice.

A glacier is a wonder to experience, whether it is seemingly solid beneath your feet or in front of you, cracking and tumbling into the water as you watch from the safety of a boat. Take the Seward Highway from Anchorage through the Kenai Peninsula to the fishing port of Seward, one of America's most scenic drives. From here boats take visitors out to see the fjords and glaciers of Kenai, stopping on the way to look for seals basking on the rocks, for sea eagles soaring, and for porpoises and whales cutting through the waves. The Kenai Fjords are composed of scenic icebound landscapes in which salt spray mixes with mountain mist.

Located on the southeastern Kenai Peninsula, the national park is a pristine and unspoilt land supporting many unaltered natural environments and ecosystems. The fjords are long, steep-sided, glacier-carved valleys that have become filled with ocean waters. A huge mountain platform rises a full mile above this dramatic and beautiful coastline. But perhaps the greatest thrill to the senses comes from hearing signs of life from something bigger than any of Alaska's warm-blooded creatures – the breathing of a glacier.

To bob on a boat with silenced engines and hear only the straining of the moving mountains of ice, several stories high, and then hear the giant firecracker that accompanies a block the size of a house as it plunges and thunders into the sea… that is to experience one of the natural wonders of the world. To feel our Earth moving, growing, and to know that no matter what man does, he is powerless against the might of the planet.

Baltoro Glacier

The Himalaya may contain the world's highest summit but, 932 miles west of Everest, the Karakoram Range of northern Pakistan features the greatest density of truly massive mountains – 60 of them more than 24,600ft tall. At their heart crouches the Baltoro Glacier, flanked by four of only ten peaks in the world that top 8,000m, or 26,247ft.

The village of Askole is gateway to 'the collision of continents', an extraordinary confluence of mountain ranges where the Himalaya, Karakoram, Hindu Kush, and Pamir plough into one another relentlessly

The glacier measures between 35 and 40 miles long, depending on the season and a given year's glacial retreat, which makes it one of the longest glaciers outside the polar regions. It is fed by a series of tributaries, including the mighty Godwin Austen Glacier, flowing south from K2, the Abruzzi Glacier and Gasherbrum Glaciers, running off the collection of Gasherbrum peaks, and the Yermandendu Glacier, pouring off Masherbrum. Among the surrounding colossi are K2 (at 28,251ft the world's second tallest mountain), Gasherbrums I, II, III, and IV, Broad Peak, and Masherbrum, which is the original K1 – K standing for Karakoram. At its base, the Baltoro Glacier gives rise to the Shigar River, a major artery of the great Indus.

Reaching Baltoro is an extreme journey itself. North of Islamabad, where temperatures regularly exceed 100°F, you find yourself on the Karakoram Highway. This incredible feat of engineering took nearly 30 years to complete and is one of the highest international road crossings in the world. From Havelian in

Pakistan to Kashgar in China's Xinjiang province, the road stretches over 746 miles and, such was the physical hardship incurred grinding a way through the frozen rock, one Chinese workman is said to have perished for every mile completed. The Karakoram Highway crawls up an arm of the old Silk Road to Gilgit, growing colder with every few feet and passing the ninth highest mountain in the world, Nanga Parbat (26,657ft), en route. From Gilgit, even more precarious tracks take you to Skardu, the capital of Baltistan and, further on, the remote village of Askole, gateway to what has been termed the collision of continents, an extraordinary confluence of mountain ranges where the Himalaya, Karakoram, Hindu Kush, and Pamir plough into one another relentlessly, driven on by their underlying tectonic plates.

The trough of the glacier is broad and its center is a vast snowfield. Small valley glaciers form icefalls where they meet the trunk glacier, and the sidewalls vary from very steep to precipitous. Most visitors spend a week trekking the Baltoro corridor, each day bringing new peaks into view: Paiyu 'Salt' Peak, Cathedral Spires, Great Trango Towers, and Muztagh Tower. The Trango Towers (20,624ft) are hard to believe, their vertical faces forming the world's tallest cliffs. The sheer sides of Muztagh Tower have been likened to the head of an axe driven into the shoulder of the northern ridge. The glacier has also carved striations on the surrounding rocks, while ice flows have formed depressions that serve as basins for numerous glacial lakes. Fosco Maraini, the renowned Italian climber, described the area as the 'World's Greatest Museum in Shape and Form'.

Yet the Baltoro, incredibly, saves the best until last. At the head, where its ice flow meets those of the Godwin Austen and Nuating glaciers, sits Concordia (18,045ft), base camp for K2. All around this mighty bowl are thrusting spikes of granite, none more spectacular than the twisting skewer of Mitre Peak. The king, K2, dominates to the north, unconquered until Professor Ardito Desio's Italian expedition in 1954. Its local name is Chogori (Savage Peak), and the crest of its queen, Chogolisa (Bride's Peak), sits elegantly to the south.

Up above, the clouds rip apart to reveal an expanse of pure azure. The glare from the ice can be blinding but the weather is in constant flux and scorching heat can soon be replaced by the blast of a sandstorm or a blizzard. If you are lucky, an evening's sunset might cast its serene glow across the Shining Wall of the Gasherbrums as you hunker down for the night.

There are infinite opportunities for 8,000m climbs, first ascents, and magnificent treks in the Karakoram, yet only about 1,500 climbers and trekkers visit the region annually. Indeed, the entire region is sparsely populated. Those that are here, the indigenous Balti, arrived from Tibet some 600 to 800 years ago. Their language is common to the Himalayan Sherpa, but their culture is radically different. In the sixteenth century, all traces of Buddhism were purged by the Moguls and replaced with the stricter codes of Islam. You will find no alcohol here, or teahouses for that matter, but in their stead you will be able to feast on goat curry and sweet chai, while five times a day the air around you is filled with the muezzin's ghostly call to prayer. (There's no need for a toothbrush, by the way, because the silt in the water grinds away any plaque.)

Over the centuries, many of Asia's great explorers have ventured through the Karakoram, especially during the Great Game, the political battle between Russia and Britain that took place at the end of the nineteenth century and the beginning of the twentieth. Their 'leader' was Sir Francis Younghusband, later head of the infamous mission to Tibet in 1903–4, and the first European to cross the range via the Mustagh Pass, but others such as Captain Henry Haversham Godwin-Austen, Russian officer Captain Gromchevsky, and Lieutenant TG Montgomerie, have left their mark. It was Montgomerie who, while mapping out Kashmir for the Survey of India, caught sight of two giant peaks in the far western distance. Presuming them to belong to the Karakoram Range, he gave them the epithets K1 and K2.

In his classic novel *Lost Horizon*, James Hilton has his protagonists' plane crash into the side of a mountain range while attempting to flee local unrest. During their subsequent adventure, they discover a valley of unsurpassed natural beauty, an earthly paradise known as Shangri La. The mountain range he chose for this utopia? The Karakoram. Standing on Baltoro Glacier, it is easy to see why.

Iceland

Geysers spit and hiss, waterfalls thunder, foam, and froth, and steaming sulphurous mud pools bubble like cauldrons – Iceland seems to be spilling over. Here the rawest forces of nature collide, collapse, and cascade. Perched in the Atlantic Ocean just below the Arctic Circle, Iceland is a geological tour de force, a testament to the power of Mother Nature. It shows in full strength just what the Earth's elemental energy can create when left to rock, roll, and rumble. Volcanoes explode, glaciers shift, and the core of the Earth feels alive and kicking. What has been left is a drama-loaded landscape of glacial-hewn valleys, remote rugged mountains, and a sea of seemingly endless lava fields. Nowhere else can you see such diversity of natural phenomena and in such close proximity. On an island less than half the size of Great Britain, you could be walking on a glacier in the morning and by afternoon be peering into the magma chamber of a volcano.

The earliest recorded visitor, a Norwegian Viking named Flóki Vilgerdarson, attempted to settle the land in 864. Winter brought harsh arctic weather, and his cattle perished in the snowy wastes. Forced to leave, he named the island Ice-land. With more than 11 per cent of the country being covered in ice, it certainly does justice to the name, and now visitors come to Iceland just because of its ice. At more than 3,243 square miles, the Vatnajökull ice cap is larger than

> Iceland is a geological tour de force, a testament to the power of Mother Nature. It shows in full strength just what the Earth's most elemental energy can create when left to rock, roll, and rumble

all the glaciers in Europe combined. From its snow-packed crest, in places more than 3,280ft thick, scores of glaciers slide downward – twists of braided ice that look like clawing frozen fingers.

Dominating the southeast corner of Iceland, the ice cap is the draw card of the Skaftafell National Park. It also comes complete with its very own volcano, the submerged Grimsvötn, which lies sulkily rumbling beneath the mantle of the ice, waiting to blow its top again. Its most violent eruption was in 1934 when hot magma and gases clashed catastrophically with the freezing temperatures of the ice cap. This glacial burst, or jökulhlaups, unleashed a devastating 1,412,640 cubic feet of water. It erupted again in 1998, and air traffic was forced to divert due to the six-mile-high plumes of ash smoke, which could be seen in Reykjavík. A day later, the eruption started dwindling and the wind carried the ash to the north. Ten days later, the eruption was declared finished. Since then there have been no recent recorded fits of temper on quite the same scale.

A short walk will bring you face to face with the front of the Skaftafellsjökull glacier, a groaning tongue of ice whose frozen curves look like the delicate swirling peaks of a perfect meringue. But looks can be deceptive. The glacier is riddled with crevasse-hewn gullies and pock-marked with age-old ice that is gray and dirty. Beneath these folds of ice are the unseen glacial rivers, running fast and furious below.

For more dazzling colors, the nearby 656ft-deep Jökulsárlon lake is choked with floating luminous blue icebergs that drift slowly toward the sea – it's immediately obvious why film-makers choose this location to shoot extreme polar scenes. Skirting the

southern edges of the Vatnajökull ice cap, this natural lagoon is located right next to the main road connecting the town of Höfn with Skaftafell.

But to get up really close to the ice you have to go onto the ice cap. Here you can feel the tingling rush of cold air on your cheeks as you speed across the snow aboard a skidoo with the lofty knowledge that you are atop the third largest mass of ice outside Antarctica and Greenland. To the north, towering snow-capped peaks dominate and there's an uninterrupted view of mile after mile of pristine snow. To the south, the ocean is fringed by the distinctive Sandur, the black sandy plains formed by the constant movement of glacial detritus, and criss-crossed with a tangle of streams.

Snow and ice govern almost everything. It is only when summer comes that the normally snow-choked interior, a vast wilderness area in the middle of the country, finally opens up and can be explored.

Dominated by three main ice caps, Vatnajökull, Langjökull, and Hofsjökull, these towering ice masses erode the mountainside with the constant movement of their glaciers, creating a desert where sand and gravel reign. Two different routes, the Kjölur and Sprengisandur, enable four-wheel-drive vehicles and hardy cyclists to penetrate the uninhabited central highlands. Rough dirt tracks take you across unbridged rivers, past mountains and calderas, and through lava fields dotted with ice-cold lakes. The tracks are dusty, the route is far from smooth, but stare out across these desolate uninhabited rolling plains and you could almost be transported to the Mongolian steppe or even a prehistoric land. It has a lunar-like quality that even brought the Apollo astronauts here for training. Legendary for its inhospitable and harsh terrain, the interior became the haunt of escaped outlaws, the one place it was thought that no one would come in pursuit. Even in summer, the wind can turn in an

instant, whipping up a storm of grit that can feel like shards of glass showering onto exposed skin.

At the hub of the Kjölur route is Hveravellir, an oasis of steaming fumaroles and bubbling multi-colored hot pools, where the infamous Fjalla Eyvindar, an Icelandic Robin Hood figure, had one of his many hiding places. Billowing trails of steam snake across the sky, briefly interrupting an otherwise bleak and boundless horizon. In the heart of such a remote spot it's easy to understand how outlaws who proved themselves able to survive in these conditions became notorious for being wily enough to stay alive.

On the fringes of this great wilderness is one of Iceland's most famous sights. Again, the awesome spectacle involves water, only this time it's flowing, not frozen. Sometimes called the Golden Waterfall, Gullfoss is a two-tiered 104ft chasm. The river Hvítá, whose waters originate in the Langjökull glacier, dramatically

plummets over the edge, creating thunderous whitewater. On sunny days it is bedecked with a haze of colorful spray and rainbows.

The river is also part of the Golden Circle, a route that connects the three main sights of Iceland and also includes Geysir, the home of the original spouting hot spring, and Thingvellir, the original site of the Icelandic parliament. While Iceland's sights and spectacles can take days to explore, all these places are within striking distance of the capital, Reykjavík, giving a flavor of the country's extremes in just one day.

You have to be prepared to get wet all over again to feel the force of Iceland's most notable landmark at Geysir, the plume of water after which all other geysers around the world are named. Geysir first thrust skyward a massive 262ft during the fourteenth century. It is far less active now, but its neighboring geyser Stokkur erupts almost every 10 minutes. Like a pressure cooker

blowing its top, it spouts a superheated jet of hissing water up to 114ft high. There's an otherworldly quality to this spot where water streaks the air, the ground bubbles, steams, and smokes as if possessed by the devil, and the stench of sulphur hangs heavy all around.

Just over 12 miles east of Reykjavík is Thingvellir. Set in a pretty valley amid lava flows, this was where the Althing, or parliament, first convened. But it also sits between the North American and European plates, which are slowly moving apart at a rate of 0.78 inches a year. Amazingly, as the continents slowly divide, a new, fresh land is emerging.

Iceland is a country of splendor and spectacle. Some parts of the landscape seem barely changed since the Viking settlers first set eyes on them more than 1,100 years ago. By contrast, born of volcanic eruptions and carved by glaciers, some areas have only recently emerged, innocent and newly formed.

Antarctic Peninsula

Enduring a storm on Deception Island is akin to taking a cold bath with your clothes on and then standing on a windswept British football terrace on a wet November evening

The planet's fifth-largest continent – so large, in fact, that the whole of Australia could be picked up and airdropped into it and lost for ever – Antarctica is a white blanket that smothers the base of spaceship Earth. Around 40 million years ago, the world's largest ice fields and glaciers began to form in the land known for centuries as Terra Incognita. They've been there ever since. Including the Ross and Ronne ice shelves, Antarctica appears as a rough circle, save for a single arm that appears to be trailing off toward Patagonia in South America. This is the Antarctic Peninsula, and – unlike the remainder of the continent – it is teeming with wildlife. For the world's scientists, it is the most inhospitable laboratory there is, but also one of the most important.

Except in a very few instances, exploring the Antarctic Peninsula is done by ship. Vessels with retractable keels are able to creep along the narrowest fjords without grounding themselves. Small boats are sufficiently nimble to navigate channels choked with icebergs the size of multi-story car parks. Larger ice-strengthened ships can take more direct routes between bays. But sometimes the all-powerful ice fuses together like a plate of sheet steel to form an impenetrable barrier that no amount of ramming can ever unlock.

The ice is sometimes the least of your problems. Before a ship can even reach the salt waters that froth and surge against the monumental glacial shelves, it must first survive a stretch of ocean

that has been described as the most tempestuous on Earth. Here, between Cape Horn (named after the tall-ship port of Hoorn in Holland) and the peninsula, the world's wildest winds collide to form gales that have been characterized by names such as the Roaring Forties, Furious Fifties, and Screaming Sixties. Understandably, at the end of the three-day crossing, landlubbers often find that their legs have turned to jelly when they finally reach the South Shetland islands, which guard the approaches to the mainland.

While some coves on the peninsula are devoid of life, many are home to a variety of mammals and birds. And some are positively packed with fauna: the wildlife equivalent of a beach full of tourists at the height of summer. Cute Adelie and Gentoo penguins waddle along in single file, wary of anything taller than they are. And with good reason. A small penguin is a tasty snack for a hungry seal. So to be able to photograph them, one solution is to lie down flat and wait for the penguins to file past (experienced photographers use foam camping mats to avoid getting really cold and wet).

Leopard seals have a penchant for penguins, which they skin prior to eating by thrashing the carcass against the surface of the water. However, it's not just penguins that have reason to be nervous of this fierce predator: the adults are not adverse to the taste of juvenile seal flesh belonging to some of the other species that inhabit the peninsula and the surrounding islands. These include the Weddell, the Ross, the crabeater (which eats krill, not crabs), and the elephant seal. On land, the plump Weddells are the most prolific. They often lie in pods of a dozen or so individuals.

While sunning themselves, Weddells appear sleepy and inoffensive. Yawning and snoring seem to be their favorite pastimes. But once in the water, these mammals lose their plump, comical look and turn into sleek submarines. Weddells have the ability to dive to depths of 2,000ft for up to an hour to catch sufficient fish to maintain their body weight. Like all seals, Weddells are protected from the deep cold of Antarctica by a layer of blubber several inches thick.

That said, during the austral summer months, the Antarctic Peninsula is sometimes not quite as frigid as some people might imagine. Sure, there are plenty of

bone-chilling days, but the endless wind and lashing rain are often the chief climatic hazards. Enduring a storm on Deception Island is akin to taking a cold bath with your clothes on and then standing on a windswept football terrace on a wet November evening in Britain. The best waterproof clothing in the world turns out to be no match for Antarctic precipitation. While the average summer temperatures on the peninsula hover around freezing point, in winter the mercury can sink past 14°F.

On wild days, with the full force of nature not only being thrown in your face but also running down your neck, the peninsula lives up to its public image as the savage arena that was first sighted and then explored by pioneers such as William Smith, Edward Bransfield, Nathaniel Palmer, and Thaddeus Bellingshausen. However, on calm afternoons, when there is no wind and a glowering sun turns the surface of the ice pack and the surrounding jagged mountains to a blazing white, you begin to understand the attraction of this remote landscape. Frank Wild, who was Shackleton's right-hand man on the *Nimrod, Endurance,* and *Quest* expeditions, once famously described the lure of Antarctica as the 'little voices' calling him to return.

Today, the Antarctic Peninsula is an important location for scientific work, and more than a dozen nations have established more than 30 bases in the region. Some of these stations remain open year-round: personnel get to experience not just the 24-hour daylight that Antarctica is famed for throughout the austral summer, but also a corresponding period of total darkness. The complete absence of sunlight has one supreme advantage: at this time of year, the legendary aurora australis, with its pulsating waves of green, red, and blue light, can be seen sweeping across the horizon to form hypnotizing patterns in the sky.

Antarctica remains the only continent on Earth free from political control. Protected (at least until 2041) by a mining ban, it is the one place that no one has attempted to colonize. And on the peninsula, where humans have a toehold, it is clear just who is in charge. Antarctica leaves an indelible impression on the minds of the people who travel here: a permanent reminder of the power and majesty of nature, and of humankind's futile attempts to tame her.

Lapland

Impenetrable velvet-green forests blanket broad unbroken valleys, and mighty mountain ranges rise majestic. Waterfalls thunder, ice-cold rivers glisten, and more than half a million reindeer are on the move. An area perhaps best known as the stomping ground of Santa Claus, Lapland is not just a sparkling winter wonderland but a wild extreme where nomadic herders live in step with their animals and Mother Nature reigns supreme. Lapland is not a self-contained country but a region, characterized by the people and animals that populate it. Its boundaries are cultural rather than geographic, defined by the areas traditionally inhabited by its indigenous people: the Sámi reindeer herders. Located above the Arctic Circle, it includes the northernmost parts of Sweden, Norway, and Finland, and the Kola Peninsula of Russia.

Each year the reindeer migrate through this vast unbroken wilderness. The herd travels almost in unison like a swaying column of patchwork browns, slowly, steadily pushing forward through the arctic expanse. As spring arrives, the reindeer respond to their instinctive desire to move from the lowland winter feeding grounds, through a landscape of frozen lakes, fir trees still laden with snow, and wide open valleys, to, ultimately, mountains and summer pasture.

Migrating untended, the herd would be far more vulnerable to hostile weather, lack of food, and attack by wolverine, or lynx. Safe

> Lapland is not just a sparkling white winter wonderland but a wild extreme where nomadic herders live in harmony with their animals, and only Mother Nature is seen to reign supreme

migration is essential to their survival, so the Sámi head into the tundra with their animals. This often difficult and isolated journey, which can take the Sámi into the snow-filled wilderness for weeks at a time, is an intrinsic part of life for both herder and reindeer, bonding them in a special relationship. For the Sámi, the reindeer are completely central to their lives, almost an extension of the family, providing much-needed food as well as necessary income through the sale of their meat and fur. Most tellingly, reindeer are so spiritually significant and revered here that there are more than 400 words for them in the Sámi language.

The migration has forged a way of life. A life blood of knowledge is passed between father and son, uncle and nephew, as they all work tirelessly together over long stretches to safeguard the herd. Although many Sámi now live and work in towns, the migration brings them back together each year and allows them to resume the old customs and traditions of their forefathers. During the long, hard punishing winter months, when temperatures can plummet to around -22°F, the herd, gathered in winter corrals and kept close to the family home or winter camp, is at its most vulnerable. The younger members of the herder's family gain their first taste of the necessities of life as a herder when they are given the job of safeguarding the reindeer from the extreme cold, caring for them and feeding them up to three times a day. Success in this role is considered a most important rite of passage.

Trekking the criss-cross of mountain trails, travelling on a sled pulled by an energetic husky team, or staying in Sweden's famous Ice Hotel, there are many different ways to experience Lapland. Joining herders as they swing into action, slaloming around boulders and icy drifts on snowmobiles, allows you to penetrate the wild heart of this landscape and really see how animal and man live side by side. Like their valuable herd, the Sámi have had to adapt to survive in these conditions. Their ancestors had an even longer, harder journey – undertaken on cross-country skies, dressed in traditional skins, and carrying all their provisions with them.

Many of the same obstacles still stand in the way of modern-day herders. While spring heralds the start of the journey, winter snow often lies choking the valleys and forests they need to negotiate. But just like their forefathers, the herders know exactly how to survive in this barren icy environment, finding hidden water sources buried deep beneath the snow, boring holes into the dense ice to find possible fishing spots, and cooking their resulting catch on open fires.

When the reindeer settle down to rest for the night, so do the herders, who pitch their traditional lavu (a tough canvas tepee originally made from hides) on the snow. The herders literally eat, sleep, and breathe reindeer. Their beds are made from reindeer furs, and the meat of the reindeer is their food. They rest only as long as their animals rest. They don't have time to get too comfortable inside their tented furry cocoons. Each morning the animals must be fed and regrouped – a time-consuming and sometimes comical process as one flighty reindeer ignores flailing arm signals and makes a bolt for freedom. Chasing a speeding reindeer in thigh-deep snow more often than not ends in a 'face plant', so a high-speed round-up aboard a skidoo is a normal start to the day in these parts.

But the lure of their favorite food, a wiry moss called sláhppu, which hangs overhead in branches like a wispy beard, can restore order to the unruly herd. In many places, the roots and lichens that the reindeer would normally feed on remain hidden under snow. Putting their animals first as always, the herders will climb trees and forage among the low-lying branches in order to retrieve this nutritious food source.

With the reindeer refuelled, the journey can begin again across more untracked virgin snow, heading for the summer pastures. The steady bobbing trot of the herd as it travels en masse, the warm plumes of breath that make frost rings in the cold air, the simple toss of a head, a swipe of the antlers, and the flash of a white reindeer (considered even more spiritually significant and rare by the Sámi) are mesmerizing to watch.

This is a wild landscape defined by its animals, its indigenous people, and the natural ebb and flow of life. Suffering some of the harshest weather on the planet, only the hardiest animals, plants, and people can prosper here. But year after year, the annual migration of the reindeer takes place, along with the Sámi who carefully and lovingly herd them, and the cycle of life goes on.

air

Gobi Desert   156

Kilimanjaro   162

US Midwest   166

Everest and the Himalaya   170

Wadi Rum   174

Tibet   178

Peruvian Andes   182

Gobi Desert

Standing in the Gobi, it is easy to see why Mongolians have long referred to their country as the Land of the Blue Eternal Heaven. This desert appears to consist largely of sky. Vast, open, stony plains uninterrupted by trees stretch out in all directions. It is as if they go on and on forever, disappearing from sight into a void occupied solely by the rich cobalt of the firmament. This is one of the world's great deserts, much of it rugged and inhospitable, occupying southern Mongolia and northeastern China. Thanks to its position far from the ocean's moderating effect on climate, it is a place of continental extremes. In summer the temperature can reach a brain-baking 100°F, while in winter it can plummet to minus 40. In short, the Gobi is arguably the harshest desert on Earth.

Landscapes inevitably vary across the Gobi's 500,000 square miles. Ranges of minor hills punctuate a series of large shallow basins, while huge sand dunes have accumulated toward the southern edge, but this desert's pre-eminent terrain is the wide flat stony plain. Indeed, the Gobi's propensity for small rocks and stones means that physical geographers now use the name as shorthand for gravel desert.

But this is more than just a flat stony wasteland. This is the Gobi in its austere splendor, immense stretches of level terrain studded with small pebbles that glisten in the late afternoon sunshine, in a region that takes its name from a Mongolian word meaning

> The Gobi desert nomads have a saying about getting the most out of their livestock: they make good use of 'everything but the breath'

waterless place. Despite this label, most of the desert receives enough rainfall – or snowfall in winter – to support some vegetation. These are clumps of wispy grass interspersed with the occasional hardy, often skeletal, shrub. This is vegetation that is dusty and usually tired-looking. It is seldom green but nonetheless offers opportunities for livestock to graze. Herding livestock is what the sparse human population of the Gobi has done since time immemorial.

Goats, perhaps some tough sheep, and the ubiquitous camel are the domestic animals of the Gobi-desert herders. Their way of life has changed little since accounts written during the time of Genghis Khan, the great Mongolian warrior, around 750 years ago. The key to this enduring lifestyle is mobility. A herder will rally his family to follow his animals whenever it is time to move on. This usually occurs when an area's grazing is depleted. Water is another vital factor in determining this itinerant existence. Well-vegetated spots may be fed by springs from distant mountain ranges.

Home in this region is a circular tent known as a ger. It consists of layers of felt wrapped around a wooden framework. The whole thing is easily portable, essential for the nomadic lifestyle. The ger can be dismantled in a half-hour and packed onto the back of a camel.

Like desert nomads the world over, herders in the Gobi subsist on the products of their animals: meat, milk, curds, and hard cheese. They seldom stay in one place long enough to cultivate the thin soil, and vegetables are virtually impossible to grow anyway. Besides, eating large amounts of animal protein is the only sensible way to fuel the human body during the long hard Gobi winter, and here, when an animal is slaughtered, nothing goes to

waste. Every edible part, including the head, is consumed by the family or their dogs. The hide is used for clothing, or transformed into leather to make rope or boots. A goat's horns will be turned into knife-handles, and the hooves boiled up to make glue. The nomads have a saying about getting the most out of their livestock: they make use of 'everything but the breath'.

A two-humped Bactrian camel is slaughtered only on special occasions. It is more valuable kept alive, as a beast of burden and constant source of dung to fuel the fire that stands at the centre of every ger. Milk is another resource supplied by the female camels. It is drunk warm, straight from the animal, or sometimes distilled over the fire to make a greasy camel's milk vodka.

Camels are better adapted to life in the desert than almost any other mammal. Should water be short, they can go without drinking for several months in winter. Bactrian camels are also extremely adept at withstanding

wide variations in temperature – from the blistering heat of summer to the searing cold of the winter months. Their shaggy winter coats, with hairs up to 10 inches long on their beards and manes, are very quickly shed when the temperature starts to climb. Huge sections peel away at a time, almost as if they are shorn off.

Camels' wool can be sold and the cash used to purchase a few modern additions to an ancient way of life: metal pots and pans, and maybe a set of solar panels and the occasional light bulb. The solar panels take advantage of the brilliant sunshine so characteristic of the Land of the Blue Eternal Heaven. They'll charge an old car battery that powers an electric light. Otherwise, life is much as it's ever been for Gobi desert nomads.

To those interested in more ancient times, the Gobi's sandy sediments harbor an extraordinary wealth of dinosaur remains, relics of prehistoric life dating back some 165 million years. Conserved by the desert's

seclusion and harsh climate, findings here have been unique. They include the first dinosaur eggs, discovered in the 1920s; two huge, fully preserved skeletons of *Tarbosaurus*, one of the largest dinosaurs, weighing in at around 5.5 tons; and a group of 16 dinosaur babies fossilized in their nest about 70 million years ago.

We can only guess at the reason why the hatchlings became entrapped. All were lying with their heads in the same direction, as if trying to escape, possibly from a violent sandstorm. Powerful winds still sweep across the bleak Gobi plains, particularly in the spring, filling the air with dense clouds of fine mineral particles. To be caught without shelter in one of these terrible storms is a blinding, harrowing, choking experience. Animals have been known to suffocate in such smothering tempests.

The desert dust is driven out beyond the Gobi, polluting the atmosphere and reducing visibility over great swathes of China. Giant yellow plumes of Gobi dust are dense enough to be tracked on satellite imagery. They often billow out over Korea, engulf Japan, and continue across the Pacific Ocean, sometimes reaching Canada and the US. Dust from one particularly ferocious storm was carried further still, continuing beyond North America to cross the Atlantic. These microscopic soil particles were deposited more than 12,500 miles away in the snowfields of the Alps. Wind has also played a key factor in the creation of an unusual corner of the Gobi, an area of sand dunes covering nearly 30,000 square miles in the Chinese region of Inner Mongolia. These dunes are the tallest on our planet, some approaching 1,600ft in height.

This astonishing sandscape is underpinned by stocks of ancient underground water lying not far below the surface. In many places, the groundwater feeds shallow lakes that punctuate depressions between the towering dunes. It is the lakes, more than 140 of them, that have given this part of the Gobi — Badain Jaran — its name. Badain is a Mongolian word meaning mysterious or from the heaven; jaran means lake. The Badain Jaran's high evaporation rates ensure that many of the lakes tend to be shallow and saline. So, as bodies of water they are not spectacular. Each tends to be no more than a few hundred yards across, edged by grasses.

But these mysterious lakes are located in a unique environment, which lends them an extravagant beauty. Each is situated in a depression, right at the foot of a precipice of sand that soars up to a dizzying peak. As you are struggling across the dunes, following the effortless stride of a Bactrian camel, one of these lakes can appear out of the shifting topography as if from nowhere. It materializes from behind a knife-sharp dune crest, hemmed in by sheer walls of sand, like a glimmering pearl in the desert. It is one of the most dramatic and beautiful sights in the Gobi.

Kilimanjaro

A million years in the making, the volcano known around the world as Kilimanjaro is composed of not one but three volcanic cones. The first, Shira, is a broad plateau. The second, Mawenzi, boasts a spiky summit. Standing sentinel between these two extinct volcanoes is mighty Kibo, the youngest and highest cone. Its highest point, Uhuru Peak, lies 19,340ft above sea level, making Kilimanjaro the highest mountain in Africa and one of the coveted Seven Summits: the highest point on each of the Earth's continents.

To sit on the lip of Kibo's crater and feel the sub-zero night air melt away is a jewel of a moment to be savored and then locked away forever inside your private treasure chest of memories

A draw for hikers, writers, and ecologists, Kilimanjaro (also called Oldoinyo Oibor in Masai and Kilima Njaro in Swahili) in northern Tanzania is above all a microcosm of life on Earth. Pilgrims who spend a week ascending the mountain pass through a range of climate zones that range from subtropical to subarctic. The ambitious trekker, determined to see the sun rise over Africa from the summit of its highest peak, must be prepared for every eventuality: it is quite normal to experience heavy rain on one day, dehydrating heat the next, and freezing temperatures on a third morning.

In addition to these weather-induced hazards, Kilimanjaro has a hidden danger that can catch the inexperienced trekker unawares. You cannot see it, smell it, or hear it. But if left unchecked, it can become life threatening within just a few days. It is called Acute Mountain Sickness (AMS), and is caused by a rapid gain in altitude.

And on Kilimanjaro, where ascents of more than 10,000ft in less than five days are normal, the chance of contracting AMS is particularly high. However, AMS can usually be avoided by ascending a nearby lower mountain such as Mount Meru (14,979ft) or, further north, Point Lenana (16,059ft) on Mount Kenya the week before, to acclimatize in advance of your summit attempt. This tactic, adopted by wise trekkers, can turn your experience on Kilimanjaro from a test of endurance into a journey of wonder and enjoyment.

A clutch of trails leads toward the summit cone. The majority of these routes, such as the Machame and the Marangu, approach the mountain from the south and are popular with the majority of trekkers. But there are other options, including the Rongai path from the north, and the Shira trail from the west. Regardless of the route you choose, it is a legal requirement to use the services of a licensed tour operator.

The lower ramparts of Kilimanjaro are ringed by dense rainforest. Temperatures hover around a sultry 70°F year-round, and as much as 80 inches of rain can fall each year. The trees are alive with the sounds of colobus and blue monkeys. Leopards lurk within the undergrowth but are rarely seen. Some 900 species of plants, ranging from hanging mosses to soaring camphorwood trees, deluge the eye with a tidal wave of greenery. It's important to soak up this color because above lies the sterile world of high altitude.

Emerging from the forest canopy at around 9,000ft, you can be forgiven for thinking that you have stepped through a door and entered a different world. The surrounding landscape initially resembles an English moorland. Then the heavy mist clears to reveal giant lobelias and groundsels. These extraordinary plants grow to a height of a dozen feet or more. Wandering among this gigantic flora is yet another reminder of the extreme contrasts found on Kilimanjaro: each evening, as the mercury plummets, lobelias draw in their leaves to protect the buds from frost damage.

The soil underfoot turns into dust above 13,000ft. But this is no ordinary desert. The air is noticeably thinner, and visitors who have failed to acclimatize properly may start to suffer. Nothing lives in this barren environment, and sunglasses are necessary not just to combat the harmful effects of the harsh UV light but also to repel the sand that afternoon windstorms whip up and throw in your face. Yet this is also the place where the gargantuan form of Kibo reveals herself in all her majesty. Trekkers who climb this high on Kilimanjaro have seen and experienced so much, but the sternest test is yet to come.

The final few hours before making a summit bid on Kilimanjaro can be nerve wracking for the uninitiated. But there is plenty to do in order to stay focused. You can never drink enough fluid in this rarefied atmosphere, so it is important to keep a large water bottle to hand while you eat, rest, check your equipment – and empty your rucksack of everything except essential supplies. Whether or not you succeed in reaching the summit has as much to do with how well you have looked after yourself over the previous couple of weeks as it does with determination on summit day itself.

Of course, summit 'day' is a misnomer. For the crux of the ascent takes place at night. Shortly after 11pm, the security of the tented camp is left behind. For the next six hours your whole world becomes the circle of yellow light emitted by your headtorch and the sound of your boots crunching on the steep volcanic crust beneath your feet. The toughest time for most people comes in the small hours, around 2am, when the body clock is at its lowest ebb. The biggest challenge can be struggling to stay awake, as you fight the combined effects of altitude, extreme tiredness, and sustained physical exertion. Then, just when you become convinced that you can go no further, you turn around to notice that the black sky has subtly changed to battleship gray. This faint promise of a new morning is often all that is needed to renew your commitment to reach the roof of Africa.

Pre-dawn ultimately gives way to a thin band of gold that splits the distant horizon in half. Shortly afterward, the mountain is bathed in the life-giving warmth of the sun. To sit on the lip of Kibo's crater and feel the sub-zero night air melt away is a jewel of a moment to be savored and then locked away in your private treasure chest of memories. From here, a traverse around the caldera rim leads to Uhuru Peak. And after a final bout of panting, the continent of Africa lies at your feet.

US Midwest

It would be hard to find a more pastoral landscape than the American Midwest. From the rolling hills of its eastern states to the flat expanse of the Great Plains, it is largely covered in vast fields of corn, wheat, and other crops, broken only by small towns or the barns and silos of the region's many family farms. But for several months each year, a dark threat lurks on the horizon. Killer tornadoes can sweep across this peaceful heartland, leaving destruction in their wake.

Tornadoes are among the most violent storms on Earth. These fiercely rotating columns of air – also known as twisters – are simultaneously pendent from a thunderstorm and in contact with the ground. To spot a ferocious, swirling mass bearing down from the sky like a devil unleashed is an awesome sight. Conflicting instincts kick in: should you watch or run? Although most tornadoes occur in the US, they can strike anywhere, usually in the middle latitudes between 30 and 50 degrees. They have been recorded on every continent except Antarctica. Unbelievably, the UK has more tornadoes per acre than any other country, though most of them are too weak to cause much of a stir. But the US clocks up, on average, more than a thousand each year. It's no coincidence that some of the most fertile agricultural regions also have the most tornadoes. The storms that produce rain for crops also give rise to twisters, and these devastating columns of air occur in all 50 US states.

> A tornado with wind speeds of 200mph releases kinetic energy at the rate of 1 billion watts – equal to the output of two large nuclear reactors

Although they can happen at any time of year, peak season is March through May in the south, and in the summer for northern states. They often begin in the afternoon and evening, after solar heat and condensation have fuelled a thunderstorm, preceded by large hailstones and a loud roar.

Florida gets a lot because its near-daily thunderstorms increase the odds. Tornadoes can also be embedded in tropical cyclones when they move ashore. But the majority occur in Tornado Alley, an area that roughly extends from central Texas to northern Iowa, and from central Kansas and Nebraska to western Ohio. This region has the right climatic conditions for super-cell thunderstorms to form, which can give birth to violent tornadoes. Here, warm moist air from the Gulf of Mexico meets dry air from the Rocky Mountains and polar air sweeping down from Canada.

Scientists still don't fully understand what causes tornadoes. They believe wind shear – when the wind changes direction and gains greater speed with increasing height – is a key factor that can cause a horizontal spinning of the air in the lower atmosphere. The warm, moist air, which was trapped below a layer of colder, drier air, breaks through and begins to spiral upward, where it condenses into a huge storm cloud that produces rain and hail. The rising air causes the rotation to shift vertically into an updraft. Tornadoes form within this updraft when a fast wind begins circling around a column of much lower air pressure, often at speeds of 200–500 miles per hour. A tornado with wind speeds of 200mph releases kinetic energy equal to the output of two large nuclear reactors.

These great columns measure from 450ft up to 1,800ft wide. Tornadoes sweep across the land at speeds of 15–30 miles an hour, along a path determined by their thunderclouds, typically in a northeasterly direction. They often appear to hop, when the vortex is disturbed and then reforms. Most tornadoes last only a few minutes, but the worst can last for several hours.

The damage path of a tornado can be 50 miles long and over a mile wide – and it is the wind that is the culprit. Tornadoes can uproot trees, hurl automobiles and railroad cars through the air like missiles, tear the roofs off buildings, and rip houses from their foundations. They can drive straw into wood, and wood into metal; they can pick up objects and drop them several miles away. Each year tornadoes kill around 90 people in the US alone, and cause around 1,500 injuries.

It's impossible to measure accurately the strength of a tornado in full fury. The Fujita scale classifies them according to the damage they cause, from F0 and F1 (light to moderate) to F4 and F5 (devastating to incredible). Fortunately, truly violent tornadoes are rare: about 83 per cent of those in the US are weak (less than 112mph). While another 15 per cent are strong (F2–F3 on the scale), less than two per cent reach the violent category with wind speeds over 200mph.

Not all tornadoes look like the one Dorothy saw in *The Wizard of Oz*. Some have the classic shape – a dark funnel with a long tail. Some resemble a wedge, while others look like a skinny rope trailing down from the sky. Some can even be white, depending on the angle of the sun. A white tornado is possibly more dangerous because it is hard to see. (It is the dirt and debris sucked up by the twister that turns it dark gray). Size doesn't always reflect strength: large tornadoes can be weak, small tornadoes highly destructive.

Advance warning saves lives, so many US communities rely on storm spotters to report critical weather developments to the National Weather Service. Tornadoes have also inspired what might be considered an extreme sport – storm chasing. Chasers will often travel hundreds of miles following severe storms that may or may not develop into tornadoes. Some are meteorologists, scientists, or professional photographers; others do it purely out of personal interest and a desire to understand these violent storms.

The most devastating tornado in US history was the Super Outbreak of 3–4 April 1974. In a 16-hour period, 148 tornadoes touched down in 13 states, from Illinois, Indiana, and Michigan, south through Ohio, Kentucky, and the Tennessee Valley, into Georgia, Alabama, and Mississippi. They killed 315 people, injured more than 5,000, and caused millions of dollars' worth of damage. Since then, improved warning and tracking systems have significantly reduced the death toll from tornadoes. The people of the Midwest have a respect for tornadoes, which helps them to live with such extreme forces.

Everest and the Himalaya

When viewed from Tibet, Everest reveals herself in all her naked glory. From the Rongbuk monastery, the imposing North Face dominates the skyline, and every other peak immediately falls away into insignificance

The Himalaya, the youngest and highest mountain range on Earth, stretches like a giant bulwark across India, Nepal, Tibet, and Bhutan, creating a natural buffer between the Indian subcontinent and the rest of Asia. Its importance extends well beyond the slopes of the endless ice-encrusted peaks: an estimated 750 million people (more than double the population of North America) depend upon the life-giving waters that flow from the Himalaya's extensive system of glaciers. West of the Himalaya, additional ranges – such as the Karakoram – continue into Pakistan and on toward Central Asia.

Of course, the Himalaya are famous for containing some of the highest mountains in the world. And the highest of all is Everest, or Chomolungma, a Tibetan word that when translated approximates to 'Mother Goddess of the Earth. The mountain was originally identified by the British as Peak XV in the 1850s when the Great Trigonometrical Survey of India was finally completed. The story goes that one of the Indian members of staff responsible for analyzing the data burst into the office of Sir Andrew Waugh, the Surveyor General, exclaiming: 'Sir! I have discovered the highest mountain in the world!' One thing is for sure, it was Waugh who wanted Peak XV to be named after his predecessor, Sir George Everest, during whose time in office the measurements were taken.

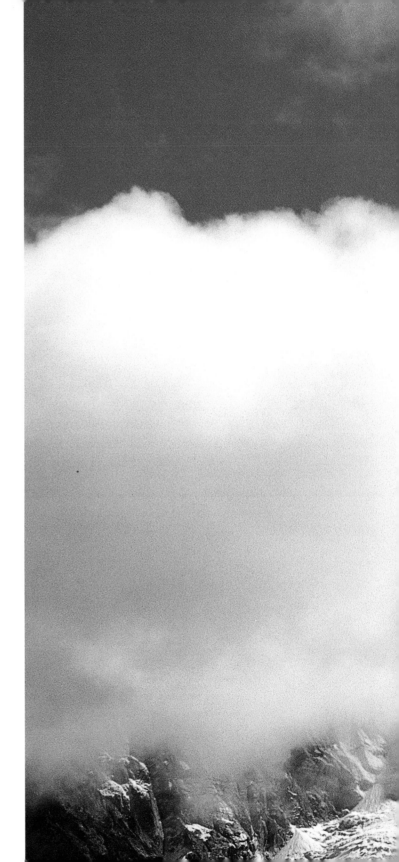

The Great Trigonometrical Survey calculated Everest, which spans the border between Nepal and Tibet, to be 29,002ft high. Even today, with modern GPS measurements, this computation is astoundingly accurate. The generally accepted height of Everest is now 29,035, 29,028, or 29,015ft, depending on whether you want to accept American, Nepalese, or Chinese measurements respectively. Everyone agrees that Everest continues to creep skyward at the rate of a few millimeters each year.

Everest is a mighty mountain. To put the size of its peak into context, its base is more than a thousand feet higher than the summit of Mont Blanc, the highest mountain in Western Europe. Trekking from the Nepalese airstrip at Lukla to Base Camp is a journey that can take up to two weeks. This amount of time has little to do with geographical distance and everything to do with altitude. As on other high mountains (such as Kilimanjaro), the main threat to human life comes from the lack of oxygen in the atmosphere. There is only about half the level of oxygen at Base Camp than there is at sea level. Remarkably, the human body is able to adapt to this rarefied environment, but only if sufficient time is spent acclimatizing.

Fortunately, the Khumbu valley that leads to Everest has plenty of distractions to help you linger on your way. As with much of the Himalaya, Buddhism is the predominant religion. Accordingly, the hillsides are dotted with prayer flags, chortens (monuments containing religious relics), and gompas (monasteries), the most famous of which is Tengboche. The monks who founded this temple had an eye for natural beauty. The landscape here is dominated by the slender pinnacle of Ama Dablam. Behind her lies the massive Lhotse wall. Peeking out from behind Lhotse (itself the world's fourth highest mountain) is Mount Everest. It is curious that, seen from Nepal, the world's highest mountain is so shy and retiring. Even when observed from the popular summit of Kalar Pattar, which lies close to Base Camp, no more than a third of the mountain is visible.

Viewed from Tibet, Everest reveals herself in all her naked glory. From the Rongbuk monastery (a geographical and cultural twin of the gompa at Tengboche), her imposing North Face dominates the skyline. Every other peak falls away into insignificance. It was to this side of the mountain that the British launched their climbing expeditions in the 1920s and '30s, including the infamous attempt in June 1924 when George Mallory and Andrew Irvine were last seen 'going strongly for the top'.

Trekkers who manage to reach Base Camp on the Nepalese side or Advance Base Camp on the Tibetan side have much to celebrate. However, for those mountaineers who are intent on climbing all the way to the summit, arriving at the foot of the mountain merely represents the beginning of a test of endurance that can last two months or more.

Contrary to what the popular press would have us believe, there is no 'easy' way up Everest. Some routes offer relatively little in the way of challenging technical terrain. But the truth is that above 23,000ft everything – from putting on your boots to ascending fixed ropes – is extremely hard work. Most climbers make life a little easier for themselves by using supplementary oxygen above this altitude, but even this shrinks the effective height of the mountain by only a few thousand feet. Climbers who have run out of oxygen on summit day, or who choose to attempt the mountain without bottled oxygen in the first place, have likened the experience to walking into a wall of water. Hardly surprising, given that less than one third of the oxygen we breathe at sea level is available at the top of the world.

Regardless of whether you trek to see Chomolungma or to climb it, this mountain is one of the most special places on Earth. And despite exaggerated reports of overcrowding, pollution, and deforestation, the Everest region remains a jewel in the crown of the Himalaya. Of course, it is not the only one. If you lust after remote valleys, devoid of any human interference, then you only have to wander a few miles from the Khumbu valley to discover places that appear never to have been visited before. Elsewhere in the Himalaya, there remains the tantalizing prospect of many hundreds of virgin peaks awaiting their first ascents. If your dream is to experience the sensation of being the first person to climb an unconquered mountain, why not spend time doing a little research and then head for a remote corner of the Himalaya? You will not be disappointed.

Wadi Rum

Mountainous sand dunes, immense red rock islands, and a night sky so full of stars there seems to be no room for just one more, Wadi Rum is the epitome of many travellers' desert dreams. By far the largest wadi – or valley – in Jordan, it was the setting for TE Lawrence's heroic exploits with the Bedouin tribes during the Arab Revolt of 1916 and the subsequent epic movie *Lawrence of Arabia* made about him by the film-maker David Lean.

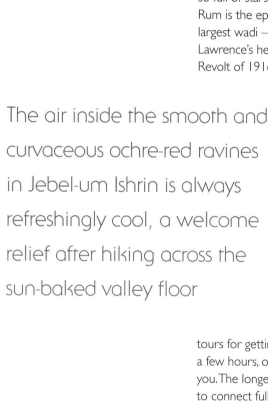

The air inside the smooth and curvaceous ochre-red ravines in Jebel-um Ishrin is always refreshingly cool, a welcome relief after hiking across the sun-baked valley floor

In the southwest of Jordan, around 180 miles south of the capital, Amman, Wadi Rum is one of a network of valleys divided by sheer monolithic sandstone and granite mesas. These sandstone islands, which reach more than 3,000ft high, and the surrounding wadis were formed by rainwater, flash floods, and wind-blown sand eroding the 500 million-year-old sandstone, wearing through fault lines in the rock.

Although the main valley immediately around Rum village has become quite busy, it's easy enough to avoid the group tours and get a real sense of this unique wilderness. There are several options, including hiking, camel trips, and jeep tours for getting out into the surrounding desert – whether it is for a few hours, overnight, or even a week or more if the desire takes you. The longer you are able to spend here, the more likely you are to connect fully with the wildness of it all.

Exploring, especially on foot, is not to be taken lightly, due to the high temperatures and lack of water, but the rewards are immense.

At the start and the end of each day the light works its magic, changing the cliffs from brown to orange to red and then purple. The dunes shift color with the rock and the absolute silence at these times adds to the spirituality of this desert wilderness.

Confronted by the neck-craning vertical rock faces, it is easy to assume that it is impossible to reach the summits of these islands. The Bedouin, however, in search of watering holes for their herds, have pioneered some breathtaking, improbable routes, which require little or no equipment to ascend. With an experienced guide – only a few exist – and a very good head for heights, these challenging scrambles provide the best views in Wadi Rum. As you make your way up through slots and gullies and along exposed ledges, the entire valley and the mesas beyond open up in a sweeping panorama.

If scrambling seems too risky, there are almost limitless hiking routes to enjoy. One of the most popular day hikes goes around Jebel Rum, the mesa rising behind the village. The wildlife en route is mainly on a miniature scale, with a variety of brightly colored lizards the most likely sightings. In the early morning, industrious dung beetles can be seen pushing unfeasibly large dung balls across the dunes and, if you are very fortunate, you may spot an ibex, a rare antelope-like animal.

Across the valley from Rum village there is a mazy network of slot canyons in Jebel um Ishrin, canyons so narrow that at times you can touch both sides with outstretched arms. The air inside these smooth and curvaceous ochre-red ravines is refreshingly cool, a welcome relief after hiking across the sun-baked valley floor. It is exhilarating following them deep into the heart of the mesa, though it is unwise to do so during rain storms for fear of flash floods. A real treat is to take a sleeping bag with you and simply sleep out overnight on top of Jebel um Ishrin. Sleeping may not be easy though, as shooting stars flash across the night sky and you'll be studying constellations you never knew existed.

On the eastern side of Wadi Rum, on Jebel Burdah, is the gravity-defying Rock Bridge of Burdah, one of the world's great rock arches. Impossibly thin and around 130ft high, it arcs gracefully, looking as if even the most delicate footstep will bring it crashing down. In the heat of the day, it is an exhausting hike along a loose stone path up to the top of the peak, but it is worth it. The arch makes a perfect frame for photos of the distant jebels and, despite its fragile appearance, it can be walked over, though few feel like stopping midway.

Back at Rum, just above the village, are the ruins of an ancient Nabataean temple. The Nabataeans settled in the valley around 2,000 years ago and became incredibly wealthy thanks to the trading routes that passed by. (They also sculpted the famous city of Petra further to the north.) Near the temple is a freshwater source dubbed Lawrence's Spring. During the Arab Revolt against the Ottomans in 1916, TE Lawrence, then an intelligence officer in the British Army, based himself in Wadi Rum and played a crucial role in organizing factious Bedouin tribes and leading them to victory. It was this beguiling landscape and those heroic exploits that inspired his bestselling book *The Seven Pillars of Wisdom*, named after one of the jebels north of Wadi Rum. The spring is a tranquil spot where wild fig trees grow, their tentacle-like roots spreading across the rocks in pursuit of the merest hint of water.

There are two main tribes in the Wadi Rum area: the Zilabia tribe holds sway in Rum itself, while the Zuweida tribe is prevalent in the nearby village of Dissieh. Although truly nomadic Bedouin are rare nowadays, the icons of that ancient lifestyle are still found at every turn. Their spacious tents are carefully woven from goat hair and offer excellent protection from the searing heat. Entering one is akin to becoming a temporary family member; outstaying your welcome is almost impossible.

If active isn't your style, there is a fleet of four-wheel drive jeeps in Rum village. The highly skilled Bedouin drivers will whisk you to all the main sites in the valley and beyond. But perhaps the most entertaining way to get around the dunes and jebels is perched atop a camel. It takes a while to get used to their lurching rhythm but the camels can get you to places even the four-wheel drives can't go. And the peace and quiet, save for the odd belching roar from your four-legged transport, adds to the feeling of exploring the desert just as Lawrence did. It also makes for some great tales around the campfire as you feast on a traditional spicy meat and vegetable tagine, before retiring to a Bedouin tent under a brilliantly starry sky.

Tibet

The Fellowship Highway, they call it. It's a simple dirt road, crossing the Roof of the World that is Tibet, and linking that beleaguered ancient country with Nepal. It is one of the most significant routes in the world because of its political history, and also one of the most breathtakingly bleak. It cuts through the Himalaya and then traverses huge expanses of rocky high-plain wilderness. Yaks by the hundred – attractively woolly, but temperamentally unpredictable – loom over the horizon, along with herds of goats and horses. Along the way the road passes through villages crowded with pebble-dashed houses splashed in stripes of red, white and black paint: red for knowledge, white for compassion, black for "spirit of protectiveness" according to Tibetan Buddhist culture and to the spirituality that is uppermost in any Tibetan's mindset. They are a fiercely proud and independent people. They've not always had it easy. Communist Chinese troops marched into their high plateau domain 50-odd years ago and their take-over of the country has been an ongoing source of conflict and debate. Greenhouses and fish farms have been among the benefits, while the destruction of the monasteries ranks among the greatest tragedies. But the essential Tibetan self-esteem remains undaunted, and even today their ancient religion still plays a major role in their personal lives.

Essentially, they are the kindest, most welcoming and *smiliest* people in the world. Nobody smiles as much as a Tibetan, and their

Nobody smiles as much as a Tibetan, and their philosophy is that they have nothing to offer others except unlimited friendship and smiles

philosophy is that they have nothing to offer except friendship and smiles. This is despite living in one of the most inhospitable climates in the world. For months on end, temperatures remain below freezing on the high plateaus. Water is at a premium so Tibetans have learned largely to live without it, apart from using it for basic cooking and drinking. Their clothing is necessarily practical: they wear thick hide coats over a multitude of other garments, including ubiquitous striped woven aprons for the women. Invariably they have an arm out of one sleeve – an efficient method of dealing with variation in temperature.

The high point of Tibet is, literally, Mount Everest. Beneath its northern ramparts, the Rongbuk monastery is remote and austere, but it does now have a guest-house of sorts for visitors (try to avoid the yak butter tea if you have a delicate stomach). Climb up to the base-camp moraine and savor the view that Tenzing and Hillary didn't have, because they went from the other side: it's best from the Tibetan side. It was from here that the Chinese made their own climb on the world's highest mountain, building a road to enable them to get all their gear there with minimal effort. Chinese engineering is also evident on the high passes, with roads that zig-zag down precipitous mountainsides to dizzying effect, before reaching out across those endless plains.

Every town has its temple, and the Buddhist chant of *Om mani padi hom* not only echoes through every street, but is etched into prayer-wall stones approaching the monasteries on every hill. Tibetans are profoundly devout, and when they're not walking round temples spinning the endless prayer wheels that surround the walls, they sit outside their houses whirling miniature hand-held versions. At some monasteries young monks in ochre and saffron robes gather under the fruit trees and "debate" – hurling philosophical concepts at each other and waiting for replies. This is serious business and they shout and gesticulate at each other with a vehemence that would put the fear of – er – Buddha into most people, but it is all part of their religious learning curve. In other holy establishments, monks sit in semi-darkness, lit only by yak-butter oil lamps, hand-writing scriptures on parchments that will be added to the thousands already stored on floor-to-ceiling shelves.

Tibet's second city of Shigatse is the site of Tashilumpo monastery, a town within a town for the monks. The monastery is resplendent with gold roofs and dazzlingly white buildings, and a magnet for devout country folk making their pilgrimage. Outside, high on the hill which overlooks the town, is the concrete wall where the world's biggest *thanka* (religious painting) is ceremoniously unfurled for one day each year. Over more mountains and across the Yarlung Tsangpo (Tibet's key river that eventually becomes the great Brahmaputra), past fields where oxen and yaks drag ploughs and the barley is winnowed by hand, lies Tibet's capital – the once-forbidden Lhasa. Its most famous building is the Potala, combining palace, government buildings and monastery in one huge fortress atop a rocky crag and home to generations of ex-Dalai Lamas. Down in the town lies the country's most senior Buddhist temple, the Jokhang. Every devout Tibetan (and there is no other kind) should visit at least once, and perform the *kora*, which means encircling the building in a clockwise direction. Sounds easy? Not if you do it dozens of times, prostrating yourself by stretching your length on the ground each step of the way, chanting all the while, night and day, for as long as it takes.

But a *kora* of the Jokhang is overshadowed by a *kora* of Mount Kailas, the holy mountain in western Tibet. Kailas is revered by Buddhists and Hindus alike, both in mythology and also in reality. It provides the headwaters of the great rivers of the Indus, the Brahmaputra and the Ganges. It is also a singularly beautiful snow-capped cone that rises like a beacon above the barren browns and reds of Tibet's dry interior mountains. Kailas is reached only by days of truck travel or months of walking across the high country. Then a single *kora* takes two or three days of brisk walking – or weeks for the rare devotee who prostrates round the entire mountain. Midway round, the *kora* trail rises to nearly 18,700ft. The air is thin, the wind is cold, the rock is granite and just being there is hard, but every day dozens of ordinary Tibetan people cross the pass on their *kora* of a lifetime. Each one stops at the great Dolma Stone, ducks under the strings of prayer flags and, with a dab of yak-butter, sticks a tiny square of gold leaf on to the sacred rock. Such is devotion, Tibetan style.

Peruvian Andes

Among the timeless isolated villages of the Peruvian Andes, it can be difficult to remind yourself that this was once the heartland of the greatest empire in the western hemisphere

When Francisco Pizarro, the conquistador, returned from the New World he was asked to describe Peru. Ever a man of action, he crumpled up a sheet of paper and dropped it on the table. 'It looks like that,' he said. This is a land that is best described in Spanish as 'muy accidentada'. Uneven, jagged, notched, it is 'accident-prone' in the extreme. The highland people will not dream of beginning a journey without asking for protection from the spirits or the saints. Even such a simple thing as a sip of mountain water or a little pad of coca leaves are never taken before a share has been dropped on the ground to placate the most powerful of goddesses. 'Para Pachamama,' they say: 'for Mother Earth'.

It seems fitting that in an area with the unpredictable geological temperament of Peru, Mother Earth should be particularly revered. At five times the size of the UK, this magnificent country encompasses a variety of terrain that is almost unmatched elsewhere in the tropics. To the west, shimmering deserts spread down to 1,000 miles of wave-smashed coastline, while, in the east, the rainforest (covering half the country) is defied only by the tumbling cascades that give birth to the Amazon. On the southern border lie the harsh Altiplano highlands and, hovering over it all, the towering peaks of the Andes.

This is the longest mountain chain in the world, stretching 4,500 miles along the western edge of the continent. It is scoured by

quebrada (gorges) that are often far too deep for the sun to penetrate, and roofed by the soaring ice-capped peaks and the belching cones of more than 40 active volcanoes. Only the Himalaya and Pamirs of Asia rise higher than the Andes, and Peru's Mount Huascarán (which soars to 22,440ft above sea level) is the world's tallest tropical mountain.

The jungle valleys might be drenched in thick cloud-forest, but trekking through the páramo highlands – wide barren plains – you find only tough clumps of rubbery vegetation, protected from the high altitude sunlight by its waxy, green-gray surface. It is not surprising that – apart from declining numbers of mountain lions and a few deer – the only large animals that live on the highland steppes are members of the camel family. Domesticated llamas and woolly alpaca graze near the villages and, out on the wind-swept steppes, their fleet-footed cousins, the vicuña and guanaco, roam free. Highland versions of the iridescent hummingbirds of the rainforest, some as big as European blackbirds, buzz busily in the afternoon heat but go into semi-hibernation to survive the freezing mountain nights. Above you, as you trek the great knife-edge ridges, a condor (the world's largest flying bird) wheels effortlessly on its 10-ft wingspan. Only specialists have evolved to survive in the harsh environment of the High Andes. And the people are no exception. Studies have shown that the literally big-hearted people of the Andes are equipped with unusually efficient hearts that help to counteract the effects of life at high altitude.

Life goes on much as it ever has for the Andean people of Peru. Far beyond the red-tiled roofs of old Inca towns like Ayacucho, Tayabamba, and Huancavelica,

you come across the gray-thatched and adobe-walled mountain hamlets. These places often don't appear on the maps and can be so remote that even a chair is considered an 'imported' item of considerable extravagance. A tin roof in a village like this is the mark of a rich man. Cargo trains of bad-tempered llamas now shuttle such 'luxuries' as plastic buckets and enamel cups between villages, and the cries of the arriero drivers still echo up the canyons as they did long before Pizarro brought the first horses to these latitudes.

Half of Peru's population lives in rural communities, and a quarter are Quechua-speaking Andean people. ('There were never any Indians here,' they'll tell you, 'that was just one of Columbus's mistakes.') Most struggle to scratch a subsistence living as farmers or as miners, in silver and copper mines, as they did at the time of the Spanish conquest. They plant their corn and potatoes – among other things, the Inca were famous for inventing

freeze-dried instant mash – and brew their cloudy chicha beer (made from fermented corn)… always spilling a few drops for luck before they raise their cups.

In these timeless and isolated villages, it can be difficult to remind yourself that this was once the heartland of the greatest empire in the western hemisphere. Before the arrival of the Spanish, this was the administrative and cultural center of an estimated 25 million people, and its influence stretched all the way from Colombia to Chile. Cuzco is still known in Quechua as Qosq'o – the navel of the world – and there are few visitors to Peru who can resist a visit to this historic town.

The most famous spot in the entire Andes, however, is certainly the Lost City of Machu Picchu. It is not quite as 'lost' as it once was, and these days you can arrive here by train or even on a helicopter from Cuzco. But in order to do Machu Picchu justice, you must approach it as the great Inca architects intended: step by weary step,

following the chain of mysterious ruins and ancient pathways that make up the Inca Trail.

Pacamayo (Hidden River), Runkuracay (Heaped Ruins), Sayacmarca (The Hanging Village), Abra de Huarmihuanusca (Dead Woman's Pass): straight off the film set of *Raiders of the Lost Ark* the names of landmarks on the Inca Trail seem to be specifically designed to increase anticipation. Many experts believe that this mounting suspense throughout the trek is more than coincidental. The writer Peter Frost has lived in the region for 20 years, and says that the Inca Trail is a deliberate work of art that was designed 'to elevate the soul of the pilgrim on the way to Machu Picchu'. Few who have made the trek would disagree with him.

You camp at night in beautiful highland meadows and wake in the frosty dawn to huddle around the coffee pot, waiting for the blessing of the sun as it finally rises over the eastern ridges. On a cold Andean morning you

can feel a real affinity for the Inca people, who called themselves Children of the Sun. But within an hour or two it is hot again and you must take the climb slowly. You chew a little bunch of coca leaves (the perfect herbal remedy for mountain-trekking) to give a subtle injection of power at the bottom of each successive pass. At times you are stunned by mind-boggling views over both rainforests and ice-fields. Raised walkways that were built by Inca engineers 500 years ago lead you under shady canopies to deposit you (panting with adrenalin and exertion) on rock-faces high over tumbling rivers. Despite the 100-ft drops, it is impossible to stop your eyes from wavering toward views that do indeed seem to be too perfect to be accidental. These immense panoramas serve to emphasize the pilgrim's insignificance, and they inspire a feeling of humility that was perhaps exactly what the priest-kings of Machu Picchu expected from their visitors.

The paving and stonework of Inca masons survives all over the Andes, from Colombia to Chile, but nowhere is it as perfectly preserved as around Machu Picchu. The descendants of the Inca have always lived in the area, planting their potatoes around the Royal Palace and grazing their llamas in the complex's great Central Plaza. They must have been somewhat bemused when the archaeologist Hiram Bingham stumbled upon the site in July 1911 and, with great excitement, informed them that it had been 'lost' for more than 500 years. It was another 30-odd years before the locals thought to mention that there was another great ruined complex – Huiñay Hauyna, the fabled Forever Young – just five miles up the trail. Rumors abound that there is still an even greater city – to which Machu Picchu was merely a gateway – hidden in the rainforested mountains to the east. But the Andean highlanders are saying nothing. Pachamama still has a few secrets in the Peruvian Andes.

life

Borneo   190

South Georgia   194

Madagascar   198

Central Tokyo   204

Galápagos Islands   208

Yosemite   214

Serengeti   218

Borneo

You travel for two days and nights between riverbanks that are an unchanging and never-ending line of shimmering forest. Two days more and the banks begin to squeeze, almost imperceptibly, together. On the fourth day you spot occasional bamboo huts on the banks. The villages seem to be besieged, surrounded by rioting vegetation and cut off by a swift café-au-lait current that is patrolled by freshwater sharks and crocodiles. Sometimes the jungle gives way to the bright green flash of carefully tended paddy fields. At other times a yellow wasteland signals ravaging by the heavy artillery of logging companies.

Such is the scale and wildness of the world's third largest island that it can take two weeks of travelling to reach Borneo's secluded and timeless heart of darkness

Standing on the deck at dawn you see the odd deer, monkey, or mongoose coming down to drink and, after five days and nights of constant motoring, you begin to feel that you are at last making serious headway into the center of the world's third largest island. But arrival at an interior trading post reminds you that you are still just at the gateway to the jungle. The going will be slower from here – the rivers navigable only by small boats or dugouts, and the rainforested hills more impenetrable. There are few roads into the interior, and those who resist the temptation to fly invariably find that the rivers are far more comfortable than the potholed dirt-tracks. It can take two weeks to reach Borneo's heart of darkness.

Borneo is five times the area of England and Wales combined. It is made up of the oil-rich Sultanate of Brunei, Indonesian Kalimantan,

and the Malaysian states of Sarawak and Sabah. Mount Kinabalu (at 13,455ft the highest mountain between the Himalaya and New Guinea) dominates not only the skyline of Sabah, but also much of its traditional philosophies. Until it was climbed by British colonial secretary Hugh Low in 1851, none of the local Dusun people – nor anyone else for that matter – had ever risked angering the spirits by venturing onto what they called the Sacred Place of the Dead. The great granite spire of Kinabalu is the only peak in the whole of Borneo that rises above the tree line, and it is said that, on a clear day, you can see halfway across the island from the summit. Clear days are hard to come by up here, however, and it can be hard to remember that you are just over 100 miles from the equator, on a tropical island in the South China Sea. To the southwest, the billowing green waves of the Crocker Mountains stretch out toward Borneo's other Malaysian state, Sarawak. Almost lost between Sabah and Sarawak is tiny Brunei Darussalam (Abode of Peace).

While Sarawak has lost much of its jungle to palm-oil plantations and logging, offshore oil has, perhaps paradoxically, allowed Brunei to keep most of its other natural resources. The Sultanate still has rainforest across more than half its territory, and it has become known as the most accessible point of entry to the world's greatest jungle island. Brunei has almost 20 reserves, packed with troops of macaques, silver-leaf monkeys, gibbons, giant monitor lizards, barking deer, mouse deer, and the iconographic proboscis monkey with its stupendous red nose – known in Malay as kera belanda, the Dutch monkey. Sabah is rich in wildlife, too, and is one of the best places in the world to see wild orang-utan – that most charismatic of apes – in their jungle habitat. However, it is the bottom two-thirds of Borneo, the Indonesian bit, that is the most unexplored and wildest part of the island. Only the least intrepid of hearts can fail to beat faster at the thought of the vast, seemingly limitless, expanse of primeval rainforest that covers much of Kalimantan (The River of Diamonds).

The popular idea of the jungle as a dangerous place is – like the stories of blood-thirsty tattooed warriors and jungle nomads with tails – mostly a product of fiction. There are no large predators in the Borneo jungle.

While most of Southeast Asia's animals can be found here, naturalists believe that tigers never made the crossing. The bad-tempered and unpredictable sun bear is so afraid of man that it is rarely seen, and the largest carnivore is the beautiful clouded leopard. Snakes are common (the king cobra can grow up to 16ft long here) and although crocodiles are not often spotted, they are never far from your mind. The most dangerous creature is the humble mosquito; the most repugnant is certainly the leech. In the rainy season it is not unusual to remove scores from your legs during the course of an afternoon's jungle-bashing. There are 600 species of birds here and more than 90 different bats, and many other creatures have taken to the air as the most effective way to travel through the dense canopy. Borneo is home to flying lizards, frogs, and snakes, plus 12 species of flying squirrels and the strange colugo (flying lemur), which looks like nothing so much as a hurled coal sack in flight.

To see Borneo at its wildest you must take a voyage up to the remotest villages and longhouses. In Sarawak, Sabah, and even Brunei you can still visit communities living in these structures – like an entire village main-street raised on stilts over the jungle. In the deepest corners of the Kalimantan you come across longhouses that are hundreds of years old. The people are invariably friendly and – where Islamic or Christian missionaries have not made inroads – social life frequently revolves around pig roasts and wild parties (fuelled on palm wine) that can go on for days. These communities still live from slash-and-burn rice farming and from hunting and gathering. The men make long expeditions deep into the jungle to spend months at a time collecting aloes wood, birds' nests and bezoar stones (monkey gall stones). All these things still fetch a high price from the Chinese traders who ply the rivers in cargo-boats.

Sceptics will tell you that the world has been explored and that there is nothing new to see, but as long as the center of the world's third largest island remains a dense and mysterious forest, there will always be an unexplored corner. For those who have never been here, Borneo's heart of darkness is the most evocative and least hospitable of jungles. For returning travellers, there is the siren call of a place – and a people – to which a part of your heart will always belong.

South Georgia

Battered by the raging waves and awesome gales of the notorious South Atlantic Ocean and a thousand miles from anywhere, South Georgia is an island few people would want to call home. This is, however, good news for the thousands of penguins, seals, and other creatures that do live here and which, together with the dramatic mountain landscapes, are helping to put South Georgia on many travellers' wilderness wish list.

Even for the most seasoned globetrotters, who may feel that there are few real 'wow' places left to see, setting eyes on raw and untameable South Georgia for the first time is an extraordinary experience. It is a full two-day voyage from its nearest neighbor, the Falkland Islands, and if you are lucky enough to arrive with a riotous orange sunrise erupting over South Georgia's dark and imposing glaciated spires, you are sure to be left in a state of wonder. Although people – including explorer Ernest Shackleton – have, of course, set foot here and a sprinkling still live here, there is no doubt that on this island Mother Nature has always held the upper hand – and likely always will.

The island has been a sovereign part of Great Britain since 1775, and most recently came to world attention in 1982 when it was attacked and briefly taken over by Argentinean marines as a precursor to the Falklands Conflict. As important as that story was, South Georgia's most famous slot in the history books is for being

The wide-sweeping beach at Salisbury Plain is pretty much standing-room only, thanks to 200,000 king penguins and the thousands of fur seals, elephant seals and Weddell seals

the island Ernest Shackleton arrived at in 1916 after his epic 800-mile voyage from Elephant Island in Antarctica. Shackleton and five others rowed the impossibly small *James Caird* lifeboat for 17 days and trekked over the then-uncharted mountains of South Georgia to raise the alarm that the rest of his crew on HMS *Endurance* needed rescuing. Being out on the same tumultuous waters in a modern cruise ship only adds to the sheer bewilderment at their achievement, which still ranks as one of the greatest-ever survival stories.

Navigating to the island must have been an immense challenge for Shackleton's men: it measures just 105 miles long and bulges out in its middle to about 25 miles wide. Made up primarily of vertiginous rocky mountains crested with immense glaciers, the highest point is 9,626ft Mount Paget. That may not seem excessively high compared to the planet's major mountain ranges, but these peaks rise steeply out of the sea and are both striking and ominous. Eleven peaks in all soar above 6,500ft, and many remain unclimbed, partly because of their inaccessibility. In the short summer season, mountains and valleys remain heavily covered with snow and ice, which extends all the way to the sea in winter.

Signs of human habitation are few and centered around the now defunct whaling station at Grytviken. There you will likely meet all four – yes, four – permanent residents and perhaps a few of the fluctuating group of British Antarctic Survey workers. Grytviken itself is a decaying open-air museum to the whaling industry, which began here in 1904. Closed for business in 1966, after the whale stocks were too heavily depleted, the old rusting buildings and tanks are worth exploring. At the rear of the village is the beautiful white wooden St Mary's church. Shackleton returned to live on the island after his heroics, and it was in this simple church that his funeral took place (he died of a heart attack in 1922). His grave is at the village edge, a little further round the bay, and it is customary for all who visit to raise a glass of rum to toast him.

With so few people, the main stage of South Georgia is taken up by wildlife – and it is here in breathtaking proportions. The wide sweeping beach at Salisbury Plain on the northeast coast is pretty much standing-room only, thanks to the 200,000 king penguins and thousands

of fur seals, elephant seals, and Weddell seals that reside there. Stepping off the small Zodiac rubber boats used to get from cruise ship to beach is like entering your very own wildlife documentary. A cacophony of screeches, grunts, and honks reverberates across the gravelly sand as penguins jostle for position, seals fight over territory and skuas and seagulls wheel overhead.

Although the vast swathes of penguins command attention, it is perhaps the various species of seal that leave the most lasting impression. Despite their cute looks, the belligerent fur seals are intensely territorial and not shy of warding off unwary humans. Venture into their personal space and the least you can expect is a sharp bark; wander closer and the bark is likely to turn into a full-on charge. There is no illusion about the power of the male elephant seals. The dominant ones, known as beach masters, can lollop their vast bodies at startling speeds when intruders threaten their harem.

Further east, past Grytviken, the beach at Gold Harbour has a stunning setting beneath hanging glaciers. It's smaller than Salisbury Plain but no less interesting. A large population of king penguins, resplendent in their black and white coats and distinctive golden neck flashes, lives here. The adults waddle around hooting and hollering, while their young chicks, gathered together in a rookery at the rear of the beach and rugged up in their thick brown feathery coats, are intrigued with all that is going on. With a little patience and by getting down to their level, you may well find a chick coming up for a closer inspection of your clothes or shoes.

At the very eastern tip of the island is Drygalski Fjord, a lengthy inlet shielded on both sides by soaring cliffs. Near the entrance is the almost hidden Larsen Harbour, a dramatic narrow inlet guarded on both sides by sheer rock faces. It was used by the whalers to store carcasses, due to its relatively tranquil waters. At the head of Drygalski Fjord is a deep blue hanging glacier, which stretches far back into the mountain range. Occasionally, hunks of ice calve into the sea below, creating waves big enough to rock even the largest ships.

Sailing away from South Georgia is heart wrenching: the chances are that you will never see a wilder place in a wilder location, and especially one bestowed with such outstanding wildlife and natural rugged beauty.

Madagascar

More than 700 years ago Marco Polo wrote of a 'great red island' that was rumored to lie off the coast of Africa. He later named the island Madagascar. 'More elephants are bred here than in any other province,' he reported. 'They have leopards and lynxes and lion also in great number.' Possibly influenced by the Arab folktales of Sinbad the Sailor, Marco Polo described a bird so huge that it could pounce on an elephant and carry it off to its nest.

In fact, only 10 per cent of Madagascar's wildlife occurs elsewhere in the world, and elephants, leopards, lynxes, and lions are not found on the island at all. Strangely, the great explorer was much closer to the truth with his 'elephant bird' story. The Malagasy aepyornis (9ft tall and weighing up to 1,000lbs) is believed to have been the largest bird that ever lived, though it would have had considerable problems flying… with or without an elephant in its talons.

Even today, Madagascar is a place of bizarre creatures and strange stories, and the visitor quickly learns to avoid preconceived ideas. The charismatic ring-tailed lemur has become familiar as the island's animal ambassador, but the giant black-and-white Indri lemur, like a four-year-old boy in a panda suit, was considered too strange to be true when sightings were first reported. The weird-looking fossa (the largest of only eight carnivores on the island) is capable of climbing forward down vertical tree trunks, and the ring-tailed mongoose is notorious for its habit of devouring its

> The giant black-and-white Indri lemur, looking like a four-year-old boy in a panda suit, was considered too strange to be true when sightings were first reported

lemur victims face-first. The aye-aye, with its bat's ears, fox's tail, rat's teeth, and devilish hands that look like creeping tarantulas, was laughed off as a taxonomist's hoax when the first body was presented to European naturalists. Add to this motley collection of wildlife such phenomena as the giraffe-necked weevil, the hissing cockroach, the giant jumping rat, and the screaming gecko, and you begin to get some kind of idea of just what a unique place Madagascar is.

On the map, the world's fourth-largest island appears like a gigantic, thousand-mile-long aircraft carrier moored off the coast of East Africa. In fact, it is only loosely tethered to the Dark Continent and has more in common geologically with India, which formed part of a Malagasy super-continent after it broke away from Africa about 165 million years ago. Since then the 250 miles of Mozambique Channel currents have done more to deter explorers and isolate the island than the entire Indian Ocean, where the currents actually assisted sailors in reaching Madagascar's shores.

To the newly arrived visitor, Madagascar still appears to have more in common with Asia than Africa. From the air you look down to see mud-walled villages that are surrounded by a patchwork of lush paddy fields (the Malagasy eat more rice per person than any other nationality). Zebu carts, similar to those found in India, ply the red-dust roads, and the light brown skin tone and almond eyes of the Merina people – The People of the Highlands – are reminiscent of the Malays. Madagascar has 18 distinct tribes, each with its own homeland, culture, lifestyle, and strictly observed taboos.

Indonesian sailors were the first to settle on the island, and it was not until much later that the pastoralist Bantu

people made the voyage from the African coast. The southeast Asian pioneers have left their legacy all over, from the outrigger fishing canoes, to the stilted bamboo huts, to their ecologically disastrous slash-and-burn agricultural system. The Africans brought a culture that was based on cattle, and across much of Madagascar a man's wealth is still judged on the size of his herd.

Within a short time of man's arrival in this Garden of Eden, two dozen species of large mammals had been hunted to extinction. The elephant bird soon fell to the hunter's spear, or its nests were raided for the 14-pint eggs. The giant tortoise, the pygmy hippo, and some 17 species of lemur (one as big as a gorilla) quickly followed Sinbad's fabled roc into oblivion. Over the succeeding centuries 90 per cent of Madagascar's original forest was denuded in the rush for paddies or pastures. In 1817, a conquering Malagasy king was to make the claim: 'My rice fields are limited only by the sea.'

The picture is not all bleak, however. By 1985, Madagascar had established the world's first nationwide environmental action plan. There are currently 14 major national parks and many more protected areas, covering the whole range of desert, savannah, rainforest, deciduous forest, limestone plateaus, and tropical islands that make up what the World Wildlife Federation has called the world's number one biodiversity hot spot.

Throughout the millions of years of its isolation, Madagascar has experienced a virtual explosion of life that is unparalleled almost anywhere in the world. Mainland Africa is justly proud of its mighty baobab tree but Madagascar has eight separate species. There are 130 types of palm and more than 300 species of reptile (including more than 70 snakes and 63 chameleons). There are more than 30 species of tenrec here (like long-legged hedgehogs). The key to the success of many of these is record-breaking breeding: one tenrec species

can give birth to up to 25 offspring at a time, and another is the world's most precocious mammal, reaching sexual maturity within just 35 days of birth.

The animals of Madagascar often seem unfazed by humans. Walking around Lake Antanovo in the far north, you will see the sacred crocodiles, gorged and fattened on the offerings of villagers who believe that the reptiles are the spirits of drowned people. Few Malagasy would harm a snake and, consequently, all over the island the serpents are unbelievably confident. Often they do not even bother to move off the jungle path when they hear someone coming – you are likely to see more snakes in two weeks in Madagascar than you might spot in a lifetime in other tropical countries.

Chameleons are also revered. Malagasy believe that, because their eyes turn in all directions, they can see into the past, and many – like the 2-ft-long Parson's chameleon and the tiny Brookesia, the length of a human fingernail – were considered nothing less than deities. Normally masters of disguise, the chameleons of Madagascar seem to be either so tame or so bold that they are remarkably easy to spot. Everywhere you look they stick up from prominent branches like large green thumbs. With brightly colored day geckos also always on show, it is not unusual to spot a dozen different reptiles within the course of a half-hour stroll. Day geckos have been described as the living jewels of Madagascar, and the crown jewel has to be the greater Madagascar day gecko – an 8-inch emerald dagger with a dozen bright rubies sprinkled down its back.

But the lemurs are the real stars of this wildlife extravaganza. The presence of at least 67 species of primates on a single island is almost enough to confound the laws of nature but, without competition from monkeys and apes, the lemurs were never forced to evolve beyond the stage of primitive primates. Instead, they specialized to fill every possible niche and habitat. The recently discovered golden bamboo lemur is a dramatic example: it lives almost entirely on poisonous bamboo and each day it consumes 12 times the amount of cyanide needed to kill an animal of its size. The pygmy mouse-lemur (not much bigger than a pygmy mouse) was lost to science for more than 100 years until it was rediscovered in the early 1990s.

In the late eighteenth century, the French naturalist Joseph Philibert Commerson reported that: '…here nature seems to have withdrawn into a private sanctuary in order to work on designs which are different from those created elsewhere. At every step you are met by the most bizarre and wonderful forms.' More than 200 years later, visitors who make a safari to the Great Red Island are just as likely to return home with a handful of stories that their Western contemporaries will find difficult to believe.

Central Tokyo

Tokyo is as slippery as a fish – the kind of fish you want to slit open, chop up into small pieces, and eat raw on a ball of rice with a dash of wasabi and soy, so you know how it tastes. But this city refuses to be so easily pinned down. Some people imagine Tokyo lying at the foot of snow-capped Mount Fuji, covered in falling cherry blossoms and ancient temples. Others see it as a crowded futuristic metropolis encrusted with neon, where Goth-punk teens play with miniscule electronic gadgets. The two ideas seem hundreds of years apart. In reality, Tokyo is a far more incongruous blend of the two. The coexistence of the modern and traditional gives it a quirky flavor, creating a stage for extremes and contradictions in everyday life: girls dressed in their best kimonos eat hamburgers in McDonalds; people can be seen politely bowing to ATMs; and tranquil wooden teahouses contrast against a sky strangled in overhead power lines.

But in certain pockets of Tokyo, the ratio of modern to traditional influences is noticeably unbalanced. When the radical Emperor Meiji opened Japan's doors to the West in 1868, after a history of complete isolation, he moved the capital from Kyoto to Edo, now known as Tokyo. Since Meiji's rule, Japan has been modernized at a frantic pace, and some parts of Tokyo have spawned a cityscape unlike anywhere in the West. Central Tokyo is a place that scrambles the senses. Neon splashes

Crowds spill out of Shibuya station and swamp the sidewalks at Hachiko, where six-story digital screens flash J-pop and advertisements onto the retinas of those waiting to cross the road

the sky with light, flashing from every surface in a series of unconnected messages. Shops sell bizarre only-in-Japan goods, such as leg glue, designed to keep schoolgirls' socks at the perfect height, and square watermelons, cultivated for decorative purposes only. A cacophony of bands belt out harmonies at train stations, competing in volume – of their hair as well as their music. Fishmongers bellow 'Irasshai!' ('Welcome!') to customers, over vivid slabs of purple octopus on ice. A rattle of metal balls and jaunty electronic music blares from garish pachinko parlors, where gamblers sit entranced in the rainbow-lit fug. Steaming bowls of ramen noodles are shovelled in and slurped down at high counters designed for standing-room only. Back streets sizzle with takoyaki, perfect spheres of octopus in batter. Over the top of it all, a blur of twinkly music like Disney on drugs indicates the passing of trains.

Tokyo heaves with 12 million people, nowhere more densely crowded than in areas such as Shinjuku. Walking in this part of the city is like spending the day in a packed elevator. Two million commuters swarm through Shinjuku station daily, piling into punctual trains and remaining ostensibly nonchalant about the snarl of body parts in the carriage – having donned neat surgical masks to avoid contamination. From Shinjuku's frenzied skyscraper district, it's three smooth stops along the central Yamanote train line to Shibuya station, the center of youth culture in Japan, frequented by young girls known as ganguros with dyed-blonde hair, deep California-girl tans, teensy miniskirts, and enormous disposable incomes.

Crowds spill out of Shibuya station and swamp the sidewalks at Hachiko, where six-story digital screens flash J-pop and advertisements onto the retinas of those waiting to cross the road. Despite the glut of bodies, no one will set foot on the crossing until the lights have changed because of the Wa, a cultural value that ripples beneath every aspect of life in Japan, emphasizing harmony within a group. After three minutes, the cars stop, and pedestrians surge across the intersection. Tokyo is not for the claustrophobic or agoraphobic, or even, for that matter, someone with a slight headache.

If you do develop a sudden urge for a cup of tea and a lie down in central Tokyo, do not fear. In Shibuya's Love Hotel Hill, you can book a room for a quick catnap at any time of the day or night. The love hotel is a modern Japanese phenomenon, a place where couples come to have a bit of, ahem, time and space together, away from the rest of the family. When several generations of one family traditionally live under one roof, and walls consist of paper, privacy is a valuable commodity. Love hotels offer clean good-value accommodation, as well as an authentic, fantastically kitsch, Japanese experience. Look for an outlandish name, such as Gang Snowman or, for the more romantic, Hotel Chapel Sweet. Rooms, which are often themed (from the kinky to the Hello Kitty), can be booked for 'a rest' or 'a stay' and, a bonus for travellers, don't require guests to speak a word of Japanese since the process is spiffily automated. A room menu on the wall shows pictures of the rooms available, you press the button next to the room you like, pay the fee, and the door key is released. It's a lot cheaper than staying in a lifeless chain hotel, and much more comfortable than staying in a capsule hotel, where lonely businessmen spend the night in coffin-sized pods, stacked together like bees in a hive.

Radiating out from Shibuya is a grand boulevard called Omotesando-dori – dubbed the Champs Elysées of Tokyo – where big names like Louis Vuitton, Gucci, and Prada flaunt their wares in obscenely large shiny buildings. The boulevard climbs uphill to Harajuku where, on Sundays, Tokyo's most intimidating youths assume control of the entrance to Yoyogi Park. Dressed in cosplay (from costume and play), as characters from pop culture, the teens loiter all day, posing for tourists' cameras and each other, and looking as menacing as only a 5-ft Japanese girl dressed as a Gothic Little Bo-Peep can. A few hundred yards away from the world's most bizarre fashion parade, a long tree-lined avenue with giant stone torii gates marks the entrance to the Meiji Jingu Shrine, dedicated to Japan's original rebel, Emperor Meiji. In the green hush, a Shinto priest leads a wedding procession through the shrine's courtyard. The bride and groom, in traditional wedding kimonos, follow the priest, a red paper parasol held over their bowed heads. Later on, they'll have a Christian ceremony as well, so the bride can wear a Western-style white dress, and Tokyo will slip through the net once again.

Galápagos Islands

The monotonous volcanic landscape is as barren as the dark side of the moon, fresh water is in short supply, and there is precious little greenery to soothe the eye. So why do scientists and amateur naturalists choose to fly 621 miles across the turbulent Pacific Ocean from the Ecuadorian mainland to visit the pinpricks of rock that make up the Galápagos archipelago? The answer can be found in the air, on the land, and beneath the waves. For these islands are awash with a myriad bizarre, beautiful, and, in many cases, unique creatures. And, with just one startling exception, all are simply unafraid of humans. The natural world of the Galápagos Islands is as close to a Garden of Eden as we are ever likely to find on Earth.

A simple story demonstrates that this statement is no idle boast. Visitors to the islands soon discover that trekking is strictly controlled. Stumpy white sticks mark out permitted trails. Walking outside these boundaries without a scientific permit is prohibited. Yet people are amazed to find birds nesting in the center of these paths, seemingly oblivious to the harm that a misplaced boot could wreak on an unguarded egg. But, you say, surely such a bird would soon realize its mistake and nest elsewhere the following season? Not so. Many of these paths were laid out more than four decades ago. Yet generations of boobies continue to make their home among the gigantic bipeds that visit these shores.

> The Galápagos are awash with a myriad bizarre, beautiful, and, in many cases, unique creatures that are simply unafraid of humans. This is as close to a Garden of Eden as we are likely to find

Yes, boobies. There are three types of booby on the Galápagos. The masked booby and the red-footed booby are commonplace, but the most photographed of all is the blue-footed booby. Watching two blue-footed boobies perform their mating ritual by calling to each other (the male whistles while the female honks), pointing their beaks skyward, and slowly hopping from one iridescent foot to the other, triggers childhood memories of circus clowns wearing oversized shoes. But once over water, the booby transforms from clown to killer. The same cross-eyed stare that causes amateur naturalists to laugh in wonder provides the bird with stereoscopic vision to locate fish accurately from a height of 50ft above the waves. Once the intended victim has been identified, the booby wheels into a dive, folds its wings against its body, and disappears beneath the skin of the Pacific. The foaming surface returns to a flat calm before the booby explodes out of the water several seconds later with its prize already half consumed. Floating in a dinghy on the open ocean watching a squadron of boobies filling the sky and dive-bombing the water for hundreds of square yards in all directions is a breathtaking spectacle.

Perhaps the most surprising bird species of all to be found in the archipelago is the diminutive Galápagos penguin. Standing just 14 inches tall, it is one of the world's smallest penguins, and the only one to breed solely in the tropics and the northern hemisphere. Its total population is estimated to be in the region of a couple of thousand. This penguin's call is as distinctive as it is unusual: a soft bray not unlike that of a donkey.

The delightful island of Española is home to the world population of waved albatross – all 24,000 of them. With

a wingspan of more than 7.5ft, the albatross is a supremely graceful creature in the air. However, landing on boulder-strewn fields can be problematic. Onlookers feel like impotent air-traffic controllers as the albatrosses, which are the ornithological equivalents of jumbo jets, commence their final approaches. Take-off is equally nerve wracking: they need a runway that ends in a cliff with a long drop, as well as an onshore wind.

By contrast, the flightless cormorant is instantly recognizable thanks to its puny wings, which it holds out to dry after fishing expeditions. It is a classic example of a bird that has adapted to the Galápagos environment. Without any natural predators, the cormorant never had any need to fly away from danger. And since its wings made fishing less efficient, natural selection gradually shrank them. The flightless cormorant dives from the surface of the water in order to feast on fish, octopus, and eels, and is found nowhere else on Earth.

But the Galápagos is not just about birds. The islets are teeming with other wildlife. Every morning, shortly after sunrise, it is possible to see hundreds of what for all the world look like pint-sized gray dinosaurs squatting motionless on black lava rock. These are cold-blooded marine iguanas, the world's only sea-borne lizard. After soaking up the scorching rays of the equatorial sun and raising their body temperature to a tolerable level, they plunge into the cool waters of the Humboldt and Cromwell currents to feed on red and green algae. Snorkelling with marine iguanas is a mesmerizing experience, eclipsed only by incursions from juvenile sea lions whose curiosity about humans apparently knows no bounds. These aquatic teenagers will often hurtle head-on toward unsuspecting divers before veering away at the very last moment. While visitors to the Galápagos are requested to keep a reasonable distance from wildlife, it is often impossible to prevent a playful

sea lion from gently bumping its snout against your mask. On land, it is easy to mistake a dozing Galápagos fur seal for a boulder and, after just a few days, to become blasé about sightings of magnificent frigatebird chicks nesting in shrubs at shoulder height. Incandescent Sally Lightfoot crabs jump from rock to rock, ochre land iguanas feast on the fruit of the Opuntia cactus, and female Galápagos green turtles laboriously haul themselves ashore to lay batches of precious eggs. And all of this happens without the slightest attention being paid to humans standing only a short distance away.

However, there is one creature that knows only too well the potential threat that man poses. The iconic species of the Galápagos, the giant tortoise, will go to great lengths to avoid contact with Homo sapiens. Tortoises were once harvested for their fat. This was rendered into oil, which was subsequently used to fuel street lamps on the mainland. In addition, sailors soon

discovered the giant tortoise's ability to survive for months without food or water. As a result, hundreds of tortoises were stacked into passing boats to provide mariners with fresh meat on long voyages: one can only imagine the horror felt by a young lad sent aboard to scrub a ship's hold at journey's end at finding a surviving giant tortoise lumbering out of the gloom.

Despite the widespread slaughter of the giant tortoise, we are still able to come face to face with this extraordinary beast. Thanks to the hard work of scientists working at the Charles Darwin Research Station, the majority of the original 14 subspecies of giant tortoise can still be found in the islands today. Their average lifespan is believed to be at least 150 years, so it is just possible that the oldest surviving tortoises on the Galápagos were hatchlings when Charles Darwin visited in 1835. His discoveries on these isolated isles formed the foundation of his research into evolution, which

culminated in the publication of the groundbreaking tome *On the Origin of Species*. Today, he is remembered throughout the islands in the form of 13 species of finch, collectively known as Darwin's finches.

The islands' relative isolation is not in itself sufficient to protect all of these indigenous species. It requires the continued vigilance of residents and visitors alike to ensure that invasive species of flora and fauna are not accidentally brought to the archipelago. Even a seed caught in the sole of a shoe could spell danger.

Nevertheless, despite the introduction of animals such as goats (which continue to threaten the very existence of the giant tortoise), we are still able to marvel at this World Heritage Site, which in some respects has changed little since Darwin's time, and to rejoice in the close encounters with fauna that view humans as friends rather than foes. Ultimately, we are left wondering: 'Was the whole world once like this?'

Yosemite

They are the largest living things on Earth. California's majestic trees, the giant sequoias, have stood for centuries, surviving forest fires, thunderstorms, droughts, and gales, rooted firmly in their wilderness place, watching countless species and civilizations come and go. Even standing next to one, it is hard to comprehend its enormous size and age. But put your hand on its broad bark and you can sense its wisdom. Let your eyes follow its colossal trunk skyward and you can feel your spirits soar. These giants grow naturally only on the western slopes of the Sierra Nevada mountains, at altitudes between 5,000 and 7,000ft. Their cousins, the coastal redwoods, grow taller, but it is the sequoias' massive girth that gives them the edge in total volume. There are 75 groves of varying numbers, but the largest ones with the biggest trees are found in California's national parks: Sequoia, King's Canyon, and Yosemite.

Yosemite National Park is a regal home for these woodland monarchs. It is a kingdom built of granite, guarded by formidable rock monoliths such as El Capitan, Sentinel Dome, and Half Dome. They tower over Yosemite Valley, where the arrangement of mountains, cliffs, spires, and rock formations, rivers, lakes and waterfalls, results in some of the most beautiful scenery in the world. Most parks are lucky to have one noteworthy waterfall, but Yosemite is literally running with them. The Yosemite Falls, the highest in North America, tumbles nearly half a mile in a torrent of white water.

It's hard to measure something that predates recorded history. But the biggest sequoias are reckoned to be between 2,500 and 3,000 years old

Some 95 per cent of Yosemite is designated wilderness, and that's all the more remarkable given its proximity to some of the country's largest cities. The 1,200-square-mile park is located just 150 miles east of San Francisco, and a six-hour drive from Los Angeles. Yosemite was the first area of the United States to be federally protected, and it became a national park in 1890. This designation was achieved largely because of the efforts of one man, John Muir.

Muir is often called the Father of National Parks in the US. He was a conservationist, naturalist, writer, and explorer. He hiked through the Sierra Nevada for weeks at a time, and experienced its wilderness in the extreme. He climbed to the top of a 100ft fir tree to feel the furious power of a windstorm, and rode an avalanche high above the Yosemite Valley. His adventures – and the well-being he found in these mountains – convinced him of the link between nature and the human spirit, and the importance of preserving the natural environment. Muir campaigned hard to save Yosemite from development and, as co-founder of the Sierra Club – America's oldest, largest, and most influential grassroots environmental organization – he inspired future generations to protect our natural resources.

'The Big Tree is Nature's forest masterpiece and so far as I know, the greatest of living things,' Muir said of the giant sequoia. It is the fastest-growing tree in the world, adding 1–2ft each year. It reaches its maximum height of between 200 and 300ft in a few centuries. Then, rather in the same way as people, it grows outward, putting on about 40 cubic feet of wood annually: the largest trees measure up to 35ft in diameter. Its cinnamon-colored bark can be up to about 1.5ft thick at the base. Even its branches are real whoppers, outweighing the branches of the largest trees of other species.

As for its age, it's hard to measure something that predates recorded history. But the biggest trees are reckoned to be between 2,500 and 3,000 years old. 'Most of the Sierra trees die of disease, fungi, etc,' Muir observed, 'but nothing hurts the Big Trees. Barring accidents, they seem to be immortal.' Indeed, sequoias don't die from disease or old age, and their bark is resistant to forest fires. Their weakness is a shallow root system and they usually die by simply toppling over.

The world's biggest sequoia is to be found standing south of Yosemite in Sequoia National Park, which was also established in 1890. The General Sherman tree is an impressive 275ft high, with a circumference of 102.6ft. Its largest branch is nearly 7ft in diameter, wider than most people are tall. Yosemite has three groves of giant sequoias, the largest of which is the Mariposa Grove with around 500 trees. It is home to the 236ft Washington tree and the Grizzly Giant, a gnarled beauty 92.5ft round and one of the oldest on Earth. Nearby lies a fallen giant, the Wawona Tunnel Tree, a famous monument to man's callousness toward nature. A passage was cut through its enormous trunk in 1881 and people rode through it in stagecoaches and then cars until it finally keeled over in 1969.

Yosemite is brim full of wildlife. It is one of the largest uninterrupted habitat blocks in the Sierras, and the great range in elevation – from 2,000 to over 13,000ft – creates different vegetation zones that in turn support a great diversity of plants, animals, fish, birds, and reptiles. There are large herds of mule deer and bighorn sheep can sometimes be spotted in the alpine crests. The meadows, gloriously bright with wildflowers in spring and summer, are hunting grounds for great gray owls, rarely seen this far south.

Black bears are numerous. Seeing one at close range is perhaps the most memorable Yosemite experience; the feeling of excitement, rightly mixed with caution or even fear, is something you never forget. An adult male at the peak of his summer weight can top the scales at 350lbs. Despite their name, Yosemite's bears are not black. Their fur ranges from light brown to reddish to dark chocolate. Contrary to their nature, the bears have come to like people as much as people like them. Or rather, they like our food. Close encounters can have dangerous consequences for both man and bear, and the sensitivity required in order to manage this great creature while maintaining its natural state is a constant challenge for park rangers.

But in the vast landscape of Yosemite, there is room for all forms of life to thrive. And the giant sequoias will always be there, in the words of John Muir, '…towering serene through the long centuries, preaching God's forestry fresh from heaven'.

Serengeti

Boundless, vast, and teeming with wildlife, the great plains of the Serengeti roll out in a never-ending sea of swaying golden grasses. Lions roar, buffalo herds rumble, and elephants trumpet. In the fading light, billowing clouds race through blood-red skies and the earth feels both timeless and alive. This is primal Africa, full of changing colors and sounds: the very cradle of our beginnings. Here you can never be sure whose beady eyes are looking out at you from behind that grassy shield. This is home to some of the planet's largest and most powerful creatures, a jostling ecosystem of animals in which the rhythms and rules of life are simple. Survival is the only prize. Here you can witness one of the wildest game shows on earth.

The Serengeti is the setting for the staggering wildebeest migration. Covering more than 1,800 miles, an estimated 1.4 million wildebeest thunder into the Serengeti from Kenya's Masai Mara in a never-ending quest for fresh grazing. Nowhere else on the planet is it possible to see such enormous concentrations of wildebeest, zebra, and Thomson's gazelle. Travelling together across the dry plains, their massed ranks are almost camouflaged by the hazy smokescreen of dust they kick up. But the unmistakable dull rumble of thousands of hoof beats as they stream through the waist-high grass signals their approach. In the frenzied surge, powerful tails swish and thrash, the males nip

> In the fading light, billowing clouds race through blood-red skies and the earth feels both timeless and alive. This is primal Africa, full of changing colors and sounds: the very cradle of our beginnings

and chase at the females, and the snaking column moves steadily and relentlessly forward.

It's a life-threatening but unavoidable journey during which these animals face attack from predators such as lions, hyenas, jackals, and cheetahs. River crossings create some of the moments of highest tension: it is at these points that the land-based animals are at their most vulnerable. Tens of thousands of creatures simply drown in the chaos of the forward surge, while others are spectacularly snatched by lurking and strictly carnivorous Nile crocodiles. These unrivalled killing machines are Africa's largest reptile, a primordial powerhouse of aggression that can take a wildebeest in one decisive clamp of the jaws.

The start of the migration is entirely dependent on the weather. Usually around May, water supplies begin to dry out on the grass plains and the herds are forced to tramp northward to the woodlands, passing along the Grumeti river and through the western corridor before eventually arriving in the Masai Mara around June. While on the hoof, males still find time to go into battle and rut, the aim being to gather groups of females for mating. As the herd pushes forward, you can make out the low-pitched bray of the bulls. With a patriarchal toss of the head, small gangs of successful males can be seen shepherding their conquests, often in groups of a couple of hundred females at a time.

This is not just a journey, it is part of the ceaseless, timeless cycle of life. For those creatures that survive, of necessity the strongest and fittest of the species, the migration eventually comes full circle, bringing the herds of females back to the nutritious southern grasslands to calve, and ensuring that a new generation is born into the endless pattern.

Established in 1951, the Serengeti National Park is set on a high interior plateau, up to 5,900ft above sea level. Covering 5,700 square miles and roughly the same size as Northern Ireland, this awesome wildlife sanctuary is the first and largest of Tanzania's parks. It is hard to imagine a more appropriate name for it than Serengeti, which means endless plains in Masai. Now also a designated UNESCO World Heritage Site and biosphere reserve, it provides a home for the greatest abundance and species diversity of plains animals in the world. Roaming freely on the endless plains are more than two million wildebeest, half a million Thomson's gazelle, and a quarter of a million zebra.

Living alongside them are 28 species of hoofed animals including antelope, hartebeest, and impala, as well as more than 540 different bird species of residents and migrants, such as the marabou stork, the hooded vulture, and various egrets. The openness of the Serengeti's majestic plains and the lack of any significant shelter are part of what makes this such a unique environment for wildlife spotting.

When exploring this landscape, all that stands between you and a hunting lion, a prowling leopard, or a scavenging hyena are the four doors of your safari vehicle. When a full-grown male lion begins to roar and appears to be staring at you, eyeball to eyeball, you can feel rather vulnerable. The best game spotting is in an adapted four-wheel drive that allows you to penetrate deep into the heart of the bush. Experienced drivers keep a daily record of the animals they see and know where sightings are most likely. But there can be no guarantees. Piecing together the clues of animal movements is all part of the safari experience.

In the grasslands, giraffes sedately stretch their necks upward and trim the distinctive flat-topped acacia trees, while young baboons play rough and tumble at their feet. In watering holes, hippos wade and wallow, and crocodiles sit stealthily, biding their time. Hiding in the shadows, or resting in the shade of the kopjes (the rocky outcrops dotted across the plains), the famous Serengeti big cats watch and wait. The park is one of the best places to see lions.

Gently floating through the skies in a hot-air balloon is a magical way to appreciate just how vast and rolling this landscape really is, and Serengeti is the only place in Tanzania where balloon flights are permitted. Takeoff is at dawn and, as day breaks across the plains, you ascend swiftly and travel sedately and silently in whichever direction the wind takes you, with only the occasional thrust of the burner breaking the peace of the early morning. Flying up to half a mile above the ground, the panorama of the plains and the drama of its abundant life unravels below. You come back down to earth with a bump – in more ways than one.

index

a

Aboriginal culture 106, 109, 110
Abra de Huarmihuanusca 187
Abruzzi Glacier 136
Acute Mountain Sickness (AMS) 162, 164
Alaska 130-5
albatrosses 211-12
Allahabad 76
alpacas 185
Alsek River 10
Altiplano 64, 182
Amantini 66
Amazon River 56-9
Amazonia 56-9
American Midwest 166-9
anacondas 56
Anak Krakatoa 118
Anasazi people 39
Anchorage 130, 133
Andes 22, 32, 56, 182-7
Antarctic Peninsula 146-9
arapaima 56
Araucanian War 29
Arctic Circle 10, 62, 124, 128, 150
Argentina 24, 27-9, 46, 48
Arizona 34-9
Arnhem Land 110
Askole 138
Atacama Desert 30-3
Atlantic Road 60
Atlantis 66
aurora australis 148
Australia 68-73, 106-11
aye-aye 201
Ayers Rock see Uluru
Aymara people 22

b

baboons 80
Badain Jaran 161
Badwater 114
Balti people 138
Baltistan 138
Baltoro Glacier 136-9
Bantu people 201-2
baobab trees 54, 202
Beagle Channel 29
bears 10, 133, 216
Bedouin 176
Belém 58
Bergen 62
Bering Strait 130
big game animals 18, 50

birdlife 18, 22, 38, 48, 55, 56, 104, 185, 192, 196, 208, 211-12, 213, 216, 220
black rhinos 18
Bolivia 20-3, 66
boobies 208, 211
Borneo 190-3
Botswana 50-5
Brazil 46, 48
Brunei 190, 192
Buddhism 172, 178, 180
buffaloes 18
Burke and Wills expedition 110-11
butterflies 48

c

Cabeza de Vaca, Álvar Núñez 48
California 112-15, 214-17
camels 96, 160, 176
Canada 8-11
Cape Cross Colony 93
Cape of Good Hope 78-81
Cape Horn 148
Cappadocia National Park 12-15
Castagno dei Cento Cavalli 86
cave dwellings 12, 15, 111
Cerro Torre 28
chameleons 203
Chile 24-7, 30-3
Chilean Inside Passage 24
Chilkoot Trail 10
Chiloé Island 24
China 40-3, 156
Chincana 66
Chinchorro people 32
Chubut Province 29
Chungungo 32
The Circuit 27
Colchani 22
Colorado River 37, 38, 39
Concordia 138
condors 38, 66, 185
Coober Pedy 111
Cook, Captain James 72
Copacabana 66
cormorants 212
Crocker Mountains 192
crocodiles 55, 110, 203, 220
Crown Cave 42
Cubango River 50

d

Dall's sheep 10
Damaraland 93

Darwin, Charles 24, 213
Dawson City 8, 10
Death Valley 112-15
Deception Island 148
Dempster Highway 10
Derinkuyu 15
deserts 30-3, 53, 88-97, 111, 114, 156-61, 174-7
Devil's Golf Course 114
Devil's Throat 46, 48
Dias, Bartholomew 80
dinosaur fossils 160-1
Dolma Stone 180
Drake, Sir Francis 80
Dreamtime 109
Drygalski Fjord 196
dung beetles 176

e

earthquakes 100, 102
Eduard Bohlen 92-3
elephant birds 198, 202
Elephant Trunk Hill 42
elephants 18, 54, 93
Emerald Spring 100
Española 211-12
Etna 84-7
Everest 170-3, 180

f

Fairy Chimneys 12, 15
Fellowship Highway 178
finches 213
Firehole River 98
fjords 60-3, 135, 196
flamingos 22
Florida 168
Flying Dutchman 80
fumaroles 100, 145
fur trapping 128
Furnace Creek 114
fynbos 80

g

Gaiman 29
Galápagos Islands 208-13
Garganta del Diablo 46
Gasherbrum Glacier 136
gauchos 29
geckos 203
Geirangerfjord 62
General Sherman tree 216
geysers 98-101, 145

Geysir 145
Ghan Railway 111
ghats 76
Gibb River Road 109
Gilgit 138
glaciers 10, 28, 62, 124, 130, 134, 135, 136-9, 143
Gobi Desert 156-61
Godwin Austen Glacier 136
gold prospecting 8, 10
Golden Circle 145
Gondwanaland 53
Göreme 12-15
Göreme Open Air Museum 15
Grand Canyon 34-9, 40
Grand Prismatic Spring 100
Great African Rift Valley 53
Great Barrier Reef 68-73
Great Gorge 130, 135
Great White sharks 80
Greenland 122-5
Greenland National Park 124
Grimsvötn 143
Grizzly Giant 216
Grytviken 196
Guaraní people 48
Guilin Hills 40-3
Gullfoss 145

h

Hardangerfjord 62
harpy eagles 56
Havasu Canyon 39
Hawaiian Islands 102-5
Heart Reef 72
Himalaya 170-3
Himba people 93
Hinduism 74, 76, 180
Hofsjökull ice cap 144
Hopi people 39
howler monkeys 48, 56
Huab Valley 93
Huiñay Hauyna 187
Humboldt current 32, 212
Hveravellir 145
hyenas 18

i

ibex 176
Ice Hotel 152
icebergs 124
Iceland 140-5
iguanas 212

Iguassu Falls 46-9
Illilissat 124
Inca civilization 22, 64, 66, 186-7
Inca Trail 187
India 74-7
Inuit 124
Ionian Sea 86
Isla de la Luna 66
Isla de los Pescadores 22
Isla del Sol 66

j

Java 116
Jebel Rum 176
Jebel um Ishrin 176
Jim Jim Falls 110
Jokhang temple 180
Jökulsárlon lake 143
Jordan 174-7
Jostedalsbreen glacier 62

k

K2 136, 138
Kakadu National Park 110
Kalahari Desert 53
Kalimantan 190
Kaokoland 93
Karakoram Highway 136, 138
Karakoram Range 136, 170
Kaskawulsh Glacier 10
Ka'u Desert 104
Kaymakli 15
Kenai Fjords 135
Kilauea 102, 104
Kilimanjaro 162-5
Kimberley 109
Klondike Gold Rush 8, 10
Kluane National Park 10
Kolkata 76
Krakatoa 116-19
Kumbh Melas 76

l

Laguna Colorada 22
Laguna Verde 22
Lake Laberge 10
Lake Makgadikgadi 53
Lake Titicaca 64-7
Langjökull ice cap 144
Lapland 150-3
Larsen Harbour 196
lava flows 86, 104
Lawrence, TE 174, 176

Lawrence's Spring 176
lemurs 192, 198, 202, 203
leopards 54, 164, 192
Lerai Forest 18
Lhasa 180
Lhotse 172
Li River 42
Linguaglossa 86
lions 18, 54, 220
llamas 185
Loihi 104
longhouses 192
Los Glaciares National Park 27-8
love hotels 206
Lowell Glacier 10
Lysefjord 62

m

McCarthy 133, 134
Machu Picchu 186-7
Mackenzie Delta 10
Madagascar 198-203
Maguk Gorge 110
Mammoth Hot Springs 100
Mapuche people 29
Marajo 56
Mariposa Grove 216
Masai people 16, 18
Mauna Loa 102, 104
Meiji Jingu Shrine 206
Merina people 201
mesas 174
migration, animal 150, 152, 218, 220
mirages 96
Mitchell Falls 110
Mitchell Plateau 110
Mongolia 156-61
Moremi Game Reserve 53
mosquitoes 192
Mount Ercyies 12
Mount Etna 84-7
Mount Everest 170-3, 180
Mount Fitzroy 28
Mount Hasan 12
Mount Huascarán 185
Mount Kailas 180
Mount Kilimanjaro 162-5
Mount Kinabalu 192
Mount Logan 8, 10
Mount McKinley 135
Mount Meru 164
Mount Paget 196
Mount Whitney 114

Muir, John 216
Mural Hill 42

n

Nabateans 176
Namib Desert 88-93
Namib-Naukluft Park 88
Namibia 88-93
Nanga Parbat 138
narwhal 124
Nepal 172
Nevada Mountains 114
Ngorongoro Crater 16-19
Niagara Falls 46
Northern Lights 62
Norway 60-3
Nourlangie Rock 110
Nullabor Plain 111

o

Ogilvie Mountains 10
Okavango Delta 50-5
Old Faithful 98
Olduvai Gorge 16
opals 111
orangutans 192
Outback 106-11
Oymyakon 126, 128

p

Pacamayo 187
pampas 29
Pan-American Highway 32
Patagonia 24-9
penguins 80, 148, 196, 211
Perito Moreno glacier 28
permafrost 128
Peru 64-7, 182-7
Peruvian Andes 56, 182-7
Petra 176
Piano Provenzano 86
Pigeon Valley 15
Pink Valley 15
piranha 58
Pizarro, Francisco 182
Point Lenana 164
Polo, Marco 198
Potala 180
Powell, John Wesley 39
Puerto Natales 24
Pulpit Rock 62
pumas 27
Puno 66

pupfish 112, 114
Purnululu rock formations 109
Puxian Pagoda 42

q

Quechua people 22, 186
Queensland 110
Quillagua 32

r

rainforest 29, 58, 164, 182, 192
Rakata Island 118
reed homes 66
reindeer 126, 150, 152
Richardson Mountains 10
River Ganges 74-7, 180
rock art 93, 109, 110
Rock Bridge of Burdah 176
rock churches 15
Rocky Mountains 100
Rongbuk monastery 172, 180
Ronne ice shelf 146
Rooster Fighting Hill 42
Ross ice shelf 146
Runkuracay 187
Ruth Glacier 130, 135

s

Sabah 192
sadhus 76
Sahara Desert 94-7, 112
Salar de Uyuni 20-3
salmon 134-5
salt flats 20-3
Salt Hotel 22
Sámi people 150, 152
San Bushmen 55, 93
sand dunes 88, 92, 161
sandstorms 96, 161
Sarawak 192
Sayacmarca 187
sea lions 93, 212-13
seals 80, 148, 196, 213
Sequoia National Park 216
sequoias 214, 216
Serengeti National Park 218-21
Seven Summits 162
Seward 135
Shackleton, Ernest 196
Shangri La 138
Shigar River 136
Shigatse 180
Siberia 126-9

Sicily 84-7
Sierra Club 216
Sierra Nevada 214, 216
Skaftafell National Park 143
Skaftafellsjökull glacier 143
Skagway 10
Skardu 138
Skeleton Coast 92, 93
slash-and-burn agriculture 192, 202
snakes 56, 192, 203
sodium nitrate 30
Sognefjorden 62
Sossusvlei dunes 88
South Africa 78-81
South Georgia 194-7
South Shetland islands 148
Southern Patagonian Ice Field 27
Spanish conquistadors 29, 39, 64, 182
Stavanger 62
Steamboat geyser 100
Stokkur 145
storm chasing 168
Sulphur Banks 104
Sunda Straits 118
swifts 48

t

Table Mountain National Park 80
taiga 128
Tanzania 16-19, 162-5, 218-21
Taquile 66
Tengboche monastery 172
tenrec 202-3
Thingvellir 145
Thurston Lava Tube 104
Tibet 172, 178-81
Timbisha people 112
Tokyo 204-7
Top of the World Highway 10
Tornado Alley 168
tornadoes 166-9
Torres del Paine National Park 24, 27
tortoises 213
Trango Towers 138
Trelew 29
Trollstigen 60
Trondheim 62
tsunamis 116, 118
Tuareg people 94, 96
tufa 12, 15
tundra 10, 128
Turkey 12-15
turtles 73, 104, 213

u

Uchisar 15
Ugab Formations 93
Uhuru Peak 162, 164
Uluru 106, 109
Uluru-Kata Tjuta National Park 106
Urgup 15
Uros 66
Ushuaia 29
Uyuni 22

v

Varanasi 76
Vatnajökull ice cap 140, 144
Victoria Falls 46
Vikings 62
volcanoes 12, 18, 84-7, 100, 102-5, 116-19, 143, 162-5
Volcanoes National Park 102-5

w

Wadi Rum 174-7
wadis 96, 174-7
Wawona Tunnel Tree 216
whales 72, 78, 124
White Cliffs of Dover 40
Whitehorse 8
wild dogs 54-5
wildebeest 218, 220
wildlife 10, 18, 22, 27, 38, 48, 50, 54-5, 56, 58, 72, 73, 80, 93, 104, 124, 133, 148, 164, 185, 192, 196, 198, 201, 202-3, 208, 211-13, 216, 218, 220
wolves 133
Wrangell-St Elias National Park 133, 134
wrasse 73

y

yaks 178
Yakutia 126-9
Yakutsk 128
Yarlung Tsangpo 180
Yellowstone Caldera 100
Yellowstone Lake 100
Yellowstone National Park 98-101
Yermandendu Glacier 136
Yosemite Falls 214
Yosemite National Park 214-17
Younghusband, Sir Francis 138
Yukon 8-11
Yukon River 8, 10

acknowledgements

The Automobile Association would like to thank the following photographers, companies and picture libraries for their assistance in the preparation of this book.

Abbreviations for the picture credits are as follows: (t) top; (b) bottom; (l) left; (r) right; (AA) AA World Travel Library.

1tl Terry Donnelly/Alamy; 1tc Art Wolfe/Getty Images; 1tr Articphoto.co.uk; 1bl Photolibrary Group Ltd.; 1bc Art Wolfe/Getty Images; 1br Kathy Jarvis/South American Pictures; 2/3 David Forman/Travel Ink; 6 Tips Images/ Guido Alberto Rossi; 8/9 Theo Allofs/Getty Images; 11tl Reuters/David Ljunggren; 11bl Staffan Widstrand/Corbis; 11tc Galen Rowell/Corbis; 11c Photolibrary Group Ltd.; 11tr Rob Howard/Corbis; 11cr Troy & Mary Parlee/Alamy; 11br Articphoto.co.uk; 12/3 Dallas Stribley/Lonely Planet Images; 14c Ali Kabas/Alamy; 14r John Elk III/Lonely Planet Images; 15r Massimo Borchi /4Corners Images; 16/7 Nicholas Parfitt/Getty Images;18 Johnny Greig/Alamy; 19tl Ariadne Van Zandbergen/Lonely Planet Images; 19cl Mark Eveleigh/Alamy; 19bl, 19tc Tips Images/ Guido Alberto Rossi; 19c Tim Davis/Corbis; 19bc Nicholas Parfitt/Getty Images; 19tr Chris Johns/Getty Images; 19 br Ron Koeberer/Getty Images; 20/21 Art Wolfe/Getty Images; 23tl Roberto Rinaldi/4Corners Images; 23cl Grant Dixon/Lonely Planet Images/Getty Images; 23bl Mark Chivers/Robert Harding World Imagery/Corbis; 23c Eberhard Hummel/Zefa/Corbis; 23tr Robert Harding World Imagery/Corbis; 23cr Michele Falzone/Alamy; 23br Travel Ink/Jeremy Richards; 24/5 Yann Arthus-Bertrand/Impact Photos; 26/7 Peter Adams Photography/Alamy; 28c Kathy Jarvis /South American Pictures; 28r Diario la Prensa Austral/epa/Corbis; 29l Kathy Jarvis/South American Pictures; 29c Danny Aeberhard/South American Pictures; 29r Mike Harding/South American Pictures; 30/1 William J Herbert/Getty Images; 33tl, 33cl, 33bl, 33tc, 33c Ian Cumming/Axiom; 33bc Britt Dyer/South American Pictures; 33tr Kathy Jarvis/South American Pictures; 33cr Tony Morrison/South American Pictures; 33br Jason Howe/South American Pictures; 34/5 Brand X Pictures; 36/7 Ralph Lee Hopkins/Lonely Planet Images; 38c Richard Price/Getty Images; 38r AA/Mamon Van Vark; 39l Stefano Amantini/4Corners Images; 39c & 39r AA/Mamon Van Vark; 40/1 Keren Su/Lonely Planet Images; 42 Massimo Pignatelli /4Corners Images; 43tl Hans-Peter Huber 4Corners Images; 43bl Peter Beck/Corbis; 43tc AA/ David Henley; 43tr Keith Cardwell/Impact Photos; 43br Keren Su/Lonely Planet Images; 44 Darryl Torckler/Stone/Getty Images; 46/7 Jane Sweeney/Lonely Planet Images; 49t Walter Bibikow/Taxi/Getty Images; 49bl Tony Morrison/South American Pictures; 49bc Staffan Widstrand/Corbis; 49br Tony Morrison/South American Pictures; 50/1 Ivor Migdoll/Images of Africa Photobank; 52/3 Yann Arthus-Bertrand/Impact Photos; 54c David Keith Jones/ imagesofafrica.co.uk; 54r S Davey; 55l Gallo Images/Michael Poliza/Getty Images; 55c Frans Lanting/Minden Pictures/ FLPA; 55r Sasha Gusov/Axiom; 56/7 Will & Deni McIntyre/Getty Images; 59tl AA/ Ben Davies; 59bl Nik Wheeler/Corbis; 59tc Warren Morgan/Corbis; 59tr Medio Images/Corbis; 59cr Alfredo Maiquez/Lonely Planet Images; 59br Ricardo Azoury/Corbis; 60/1 Jochem D Wijnands/ Getty Images; 63tl Pal Hermansen/Getty Images; 63bl David Tipling/Getty Images; 63tr Jozef Zachlod/4Corners Images; 63br Herbjorn Tjeltveit/Alamy; 64/5 Wolfgang Kaehler/ Corbis; 66 AA/G Marks; 67tl Pierre Perrin/Corbis Sygma; 67cl Posing Productions/Getty Images; 67bl J. P. Laffont/ Sygma/Corbis; 67tc Massimo Borchi /4Corners Images; 67tr Pierre Perrin/Sygma/Corbis; 67br Frans Lemmens/Getty Images; 68/9 Bob Charlton/Lonely Planet Images; 70/1 Photolibrary Group Ltd.; 72c Theo Allofs/Getty Images; 72r Alex Mislewicz/Axiom; 73l Fred Bavendam/Minden Pictures/ FLPA; 73c Alex Mislewicz/Axiom; 73r Pete Atkinson/Getty Images; 74/5 Chris Caldicott/Axiom; 76 AA/F Arvidsson; 77tl Paul Quayle/Axiom; 77bl Keren Su/China Span/Alamy; 77tr S Davey; 77bc Paul Beinssen/Lonely Planet Images; 77br S Davey ; 78/9 Tim Rock/Lonely Planet Images; 81tl Charles O'Rear/Corbis; 81tr AA/Clive Sawyer; 81bc Karl Lehmann/ Lonely Planet Images; 81br Ulana Switucha/Alamy; 82 Ron Dahlquist/Pacificstock.com; 84/5 Aguilar Patrice/Alamy; 87tl Tom Pfeiffer/Getty Images; 87r David Trood/Getty Images; 87bl Aguilar Patrice/Alamy; 88/9 Olimpio Fantuz/4Corners Images; 90/1 Theo Allofs/Getty Images; 92c Olimpio Fantuz/ 4Corners Images; 92r Art Wolfe/Getty Images; 93l Olimpio Fantuz/4Corners Images; 93c Michele Westmorland/Corbis; 93r Olimpio Fantuz/4Corners Images; 94/5 Frans Lemmens/ Getty Images; 97t Penny Tweedie/Getty Images; 97bl Guido Cozzi/4Corners Images; 97bc Paul Quayle/ Axiom; 97br Corbis; 98/9 Michael Melford/Getty Images; 101tl Carol Polich/Lonely Planet Images; 101bl Photolibrary Group Ltd.; 101tc Carol Polich/Lonely Planet Images; 101tr Stefan Damn/4Corners Images; 101br John Elk III/Lonely Planet Images; 102/3 Photo Resource Hawaii/Alamy; 105tl AA/Kirk Lee Alder; 105bl Karl Lehmann/Lonely Planet Images; 105r Bryan Lowry/Alamy; 105bc Roger Ressmeyer/Corbis; 106/7 Diana Mayfield/Lonely Planet Images; 108/9 John Banagan/ Lonely Planet Images; 110c Getty Images; 110r Lisa Saw/Travel Ink; 111l Richard l'Anson/ /Lonely Planet Images; 111c Photolibrary/Getty Images; 111r Leanne Logan/Lonely Planet Images; 112/3 Brand X Pictures/Imagestate; 114 Russ Bishop/Alamy; 115tl Robert Knight/Eye Ubiquitous; 115tc Fritz Polking/FLPA; 115tr Naki Kouyioumtzis/Axiom; 115b Photolibrary Group Ltd.; 116/7 Sergio Dorantes/Corbis; 119tl Charles O'Rear/Corbis; 119bl, 11t9tr National Geographic/Getty Images; 119cr Panda Photo/FLPA; 119br Photodisc Blue/Getty Images; 120,122/3 Grant Dixon/ Lonely Planet Images; 125tl Photolibrary Group Ltd.; 125cl Henning Marstrand/Axiom; 125bl, 125tc, 125c & 125bc Articphoto.co.uk; 125tr Fridmar Damm/4Corners Images; 125cr Articphoto.co.uk; 125br Photolibrary Group Ltd; 126/7 Paul Harris/Getty Images; 129tl Articphoto.co.uk; 129bl Peter Solness/Lonely Planet Images; 129tc Maria Stenzel/Getty Images; 129c Christopher Roberts/Axiom; 129tr Articphoto.co.uk; 129cr Christopher Roberts/Axiom; 129br Articphoto.co.uk/Alamy; 130/1 Mark Newman/Lonely Planet Images; 132/3 blickwinkel/Alamy; 134c John Eastcott & Yva Momatiuk/National Geographic; 134r Tom Walker/Getty Images; 135l Paul A. Souders/Corbis; 135c Tips Images/Harald Sund; 135r John Cleare Mountain Camera; 136/7 John Mock/ Lonely Planet Images; 139tl Worldwide Picture Library/Alamy; 139bl John Cleare Mountain Camera; 139bc Colin Monteath/Minden Pictures/FLPA; 139tr Galen Rowell/Corbis; 139br John Noble/Corbis; 140/1 Paul Harding/Lonely Planet Images; 142/3 Jan Vermeer/Foto Natura/FLPA 144c, 144r AA/James A Tims; 145l Jan Vermeer/Foto Natura/FLPA; 145c Bob Krist/Corbis; 145r Frans Lemmens/Getty Images; 146/7 David Tipling/ Lonely Planet Images; 149tl Roberto Rinaldi/4Corners Images; 149tc Juliet Coombe/ Lonely Planet Images; 149tr Chris Barton/Lonely Planet Images; 149b Articphoto.co.uk; 150/1 Jan Tove Johansson/Getty Images; 153tl Anders Ryman/Alamy; 153cl Kalervo Ojutkangas/Nordic photos/ Getty Images; 153bl John Cleare Mountain Camera; 153tc Christophe Bluntzer/Impact Photos; 153c Jason Lindsey/Alamy; 153bc Photo Alto/Tips Images; 153tr Hans Strand/Getty Images; 153br Arco Images/Alamy; 154 AA/William Gray; 156/7 Bruno Morandi/4Corners Images; 158/9 Peter Adams Photography/Alamy; 160c Bruno Morandi/Robert Harding; 160r Graham Taylor/Lonely Planet Images; 161l Bruno Morandi/Robert Harding; 161r John Spaull/Axiom; 162/3 Peter Turner/Getty Images; 165tl David Else/Lonely Planet Images; 165cl Ariadne Van Zandbergen/ Lonely Planet Images; 165bl Carla Signorini/images of africa.co.uk; 165tc Reuters/Nina Schwendemann; 165c Kazuyoshi Nomachi/Corbis; 165bc Ariadne Van Zandbergen/Lonely Planet Images; 165tr, 165ct David Keith Jones/imagesofafrica.co.uk; 165br Ulrich Doering/Alamy; 166/7 A. T. Willet /Alamy; 169tl Photolibrary Group Ltd; 169bl Joel Sartore/National Geographic; 169bc Jason Politte/Alamy; 169tr Jim Richardson/National Geographic; 169cr Scott Wishart/Americanaimages.com; 169br Joel Sartore/National Geographic; 170/1 Grant Dixon/Lonely Planet Images; 173tl AA/Steve Watkins; 173bl Nature Picture Library/Alamy; 173bc Martin Stolworthy/Axiom; 173tr Worldwide Picture Library/Alamy; 173br John Mock/Lonely Planet Images; 174/5 Eddie Gerald/Alamy; 177tl Brett Shearer/Lonely Planet Images; 177bl Mark Daffey/Lonely Planet Images; 177tc Anders Blomqvist//Lonely Planet Images; 177c Photolibrary Group Ltd.; 177bc John Spaull/Panos; 177tr Patrick Ben Luke Syder/Lonely Planet Images; 177br John Spaull/Panos; 178/9 Greg Caire/Lonely Planet Images; 181tl Justin Guariqlia/Getty Images; 181cl S. Davey; 181bl Don Smith/Robert Harding; 181tc Photolibrary Group Ltd.; 181bc, 181cr, 181br Panorama Stock/Robert Harding; 181tr Ian Cumming/Axiom; 182/3 Luke Peters/South American Pictures; 184/5 David Norton/ Getty Images; 186c Tony Morrison/South American Pictures; 186r Tui De Roy/Minden Pictures/FLPA; 187l Paul Franklin/Eye Ubiquitous; 187c Niall McDiarmid/Alamy; 187r Grant Faint/Getty Images; 188 Photolibrary Group Ltd.; 190/1 Tips Images/Guido Alberto Rossi; 193tl Keren Su/China Span/Alamy; 193bl National Geographic/Getty Images; 193tc Tips Images/Guido Alberto Rossi; 193bc Photolibrary Group Ltd.; 193tr Frans Lanting/Corbis; 193b Peter Bowater/Alamy; 194/5 Art Wolfe/Getty Images; 197l Tony Wheeler/Getty Images; 197tr, 197bc Frans Lanting/Minden Pictures/FLPA; 197br Kevin Schafer/Alamy; 198/9 Jurgen & Christine Sohns/FLPA; 200/1 Karl Lehmann/ Lonely Planet Images; 202c David Curl/Lonely Planet Images; 202r Natural Visions/Alamy; 203l Karl Lehmann/Lonely Planet Images; 203c Ellen Rooney/Axiom; 203r Carol Polich/ Lonely Planet Images; 204/5 Puku/4Corners Images; 207tl Chad Ehlers/Alamy; 207bl Mark Thomas/Axiom; 207tr Photolibrary Group Ltd; 207bc Mitchell Coster/Axiom; 207br Greg Elms/Lonely Planet Images; 208/9 Renee Lynn/Getty Images; 210/1 Stuart Westmorland/Getty Images; 212c Gavriel Jecan/Corbis; 212r Art Wolfe/Getty Images; 213l Corbis; 213c Fan TravelStock/Alamy; 213r Scott Stulberg/Alamy; 214/5 Danita Delimont/Alamy; 217tl Dennis Hallinan/Alamy; 217cl Joe McDonald/Corbis; 217bl Medio Images/ImageState; 217c AA/Richard Ireland; 217tr National Geographic/Getty; 217cr Photolibrary Group Ltd; 217br Gettyimages/Photodisc; 218/9 Paul Dymond/Lonely Planet Images; 221tl Danita Delimont/Alamy; 221cl Photolibrary Group Ltd.; 221bl Jon Arnold Images/Alamy; 221tc Jonathan & Angela/Getty Images; 221c David Keith Jones/ imagesofafrica.co.uk; 221bc Guy Marks/Axiom; 221tr Images of Africa Photobank/ Alamy; 221cr Dennis Johnson/ Lonely Planet Images; 221br Craig Lovell/Eagle Visions Photography/Alamy.

Every effort has been made to trace the copyright holders, and we apologise in advance for any accidental errors. We would be happy to apply the corrections in the following edition of this publication.